Launchpad

Great resources for use with 11-13+

edited by Sue Clutterham

Scripture Union
130 City Road London EC1V2NJ

British Library Cataloguing-in-Publication Data.

A catalogue record for this book is available from the British Library.

All Bible quotations, except where otherwise stated, are from the Good News Bible – Old Testament: Copyright © American Bible Society 1976; New Testament: Copyright © American Bible Society 1966, 1971, 1976.

Book design and typesetting by Daniel Edwards.

Cover design and drawings by Tony Cantale Graphics.

Printed and bound in Great Britain by Ebenezer Baylis and Son Ltd, The Trinity Press, Worcester and London.

Acknowledgments

Many people have contributed to this book (the main authors of each unit being listed on the contents page). Thanks to Katy Canty, Carol Carlsson-Browne, Lucy Clutterham, Terry Clutterham, Julie Thompson, Jane West and Howard Worsley. And for permission to use copyright material, thanks to …

Eddie Askew for the stories in units 5 and 18 (from *Many Voices, One Voice*, published by the Leprosy Mission International).

Joan Brockelsby for the poem 'Hair 543' (from *A Touch of Flame*, Lion) in unit 5.

Peter Graystone for the song in unit 11.

Jeremie Hughes for the problem page letter 'answers' in unit 3, taken from *Questions Children Ask* (Lion).

JAM magazine – the source of the funsheet 'The tongue is …' in unit 7.

Link-up (Scripture Union in Schools) – the source of the board game in unit 7.

Mario Marchio (of Bosko Ministries, Cape Town) for the poem in unit 5.

Richard Medrington for the stories 'King Arthur and the Short Knight' (unit 2) and 'The Jester' (unit 12), for the puzzle 'The Blind Beggar' (unit 16) and for the sketchscript in unit 16.

One to One – the source of the sketchscript in unit 3 and the prayabout sheets in units 15, 17 and 18.

Someone unknown for the story 'The Long Silence' in unit 17.

Derek Wood for the story in unit 14.

Contents

Introduction

Countdown

You're off! Launched into the unknown with a group of 11–13s … Aaaagh! But help is at hand so that, together with your group members, you can come closer to God, closer to each other and have some fun in the process!

This resource book is designed to be used with various types of group, so whether you're running a mid-week club, a lunch-time meeting in school, or even a residential event, the material should be suitable for your group.

It deals with 'issues' – those thorny problems that 11–13s are starting to grapple with as they approach adolescence and learn to cope with their changing bodies, unpredictable emotions and developing attitudes. There's no attempt to handle all the questions about life, death and the universe (and there aren't any easy answers provided either!), but the material aims to help young people sort out what they believe now, so that they are prepared for the future and the increasing pressures they will face out in the big, wide and often hostile, world.

The 'issue' is the starting point – it's usually where 11–13s are 'at' – and by looking at it in depth and exploring it through discussion, surveys, games, sketches, role-play, and a host of other activities, the aim is to help the group members discover a Christian attitude to the subject, what the Bible says about it, and how Christian faith can make a practical difference to their lives at home, at school, or with their friends.

The introduction to each chapter gives an idea of the activities included. Group leaders can select from the material as they wish, according to the specific needs of their particular group, the time available and the ability of the group members. Most of the material can be easily adapted.

A programme can follow the order in which the ideas are given, but it's not essential, nor is it necessary to use them all. However, if most of the material is used, there's more than enough for at least two sessions (depending, of course, on their length!). The times given for most activities are only approximate, and are intended as a rough guide only.

If you are working with youngsters for whom contact with the group is their only link with Christianity, and who have no experience whatsoever of church, let alone personal Bible reading, then some of the material will need to be adapted. However, don't leave out the Christian content altogether simply because your group members may not be familiar with the Bible. For instance, the 'Bible focus' activities could still be used, but perhaps page numbers could be used for the various passages, so that group members could find them easily, rather than having to cope with looking up Bible references. (You'll need a group set of Bibles – preferably Good News Bibles – too.) An apologetic approach might also be necessary. Topics could be introduced with the words 'Christians believe …' rather than an assumptive statement such as 'We know …' 'Un-churched' young people who come into contact with a Christian group such as yours, may be hearing about Jesus for the first time in their lives. Who knows what seeds might be sown, and how the Holy Spirit might use what is said and done in the meetings to bring them closer to God?

Many of the activities will help group members to get to know each other (and you) better, as everyone learns together. Other ideas to help you build up group identity and fellowship could include:

- programme cards for each group member, giving details of forthcoming events and helping individuals to feel they 'belong'
- refreshments during your time together, so that group members have a chance to relax and chat to each other
- a portable group notice-board to keep everyone informed.

Venue

The venue for a group meeting is often temporary and limited (you may, for example, have the use of a church hall or classroom, but only for one hour exactly, once a week after school). The ideas suggested take into account these constraints. If your meeting room is well equipped, with everything at your disposal, permanent display space and all the necessary equipment readily available, consider it a real bonus, and be grateful!

Materials you will need

- A copy of the Good News Bible for every group member. (Encourage them to bring their own.)
- An overhead projector (plus acetate sheets and washable overhead projector pens).
- Large sheets of paper (poster size), especially if you don't have the use of an overhead projector.
- Different coloured thick felt pens.
- *Blu-tack* and/or drawing pins (for attaching your masterpieces to the wall!)
- Scissors, glue sticks, thin felt pens, magazines and newspapers (for collages).
- Scrap paper and pencils or biros (enough for all the group members to have one each – they never have anything to write with when they need to!)

Handouts

All the funsheets, questionnaires and surveys in this book are photocopiable, and may be reproduced without permission. You will need regular access to a photocopier as most of the issues covered have at least one handout for the group members. If paying for copies stretches the budget, why not see if your local church members could support your work with the group by helping to meet your expenses?

6 Discussions

Many of the activities involve discussion. Fine, if your group is willing and able to participate! However, if you have group members who are shy, reticent, or even unwilling to participate and for whom speaking in 'public' would be an ordeal, then you will need to work hard at drawing them into any discussion. Here are a few guidelines which may be helpful:

- Make sure the group are as comfortable as possible! If they're sitting on hard chairs in a hot, stuffy room, with the sun in their eyes, don't be surprised if your questions meet with little or no response! Sit in a circle so that the group members can see each other and feel part of the discussion.
- Everyone will be more likely to contribute if they feel relaxed, at ease with each other and sure of acceptance, whatever they say and however they say it. A few light-hearted questions or some initial chit-chat might help to 'break the ice' – and the nature of the activity preceding the discussion will be crucial, too.
- Usually it will be the group leader's job to act as 'chairman' in discussions. Make sure you know what points need to be drawn out and emphasised. Be ready to rephrase questions if necessary. Remain neutral at first, but as the discussion progresses you may need to intervene and steer the conversation in the right direction, by providing Christian guidelines. Don't let it go on too long and sum up what has arisen at the end, relating it back to the theme.
- Do be tactful with any group members who are unfamiliar with the Bible or Christian things. Obviously, you cannot ignore something that's been said if it is clearly wrong, but avoid embarrassing a group member, or showing up their ignorance.
- Be politely firm with the talkative group member who doesn't give anyone else a chance! Asking the rest of the group, or another individual, 'What do you think?' might help!
- If the group members don't listen to each other, or interrupt each other, have a Bible handy. Make a rule that the only person allowed to speak must be holding the Bible!
- Don't draw too much attention to group members who don't contribute, but invite them to contribute if they want to. It may be they were in need of some gentle encouragement! However, do provide a way of escape that they can use if they want to, so that they don't feel threatened. For example, 'Would you like to add anything, Lucy, or has it been said already?' means that Lucy isn't cornered, neither does she end up looking silly in front of the others.
- Often, one really honest person is all it takes to 'get the ball rolling' in a discussion! A few heart-felt comments can let the barriers down and soon have everyone joining in with their point of view, relieved to find that someone else has doubts, or worries, or whatever! If that doesn't happen, it might help if you can share your hopes and fears, as appropriate. You will probably find that the group will respond well when they realise that you're fallible too!
- Don't be afraid to say, 'I don't know'. If you always have the right answer, the discussion will turn into a lecture.
- Keep a sense of humour and let the group members relax and enjoy discussing!

Songs

Where appropriate, a list of suitable songs is given with the issue covered. *Mission Praise* (published by Marshall Pickering) is the suggested songbook and it's recommended that you arrange to obtain or borrow enough copies for your group, so that you do not flout copyright laws.

Videos

Where videos have been suggested as a further resource, it is *essential* that you watch them in advance, before showing them to your group. If you don't have access to a video recorder and television, they should be easy enough to borrow for your meeting, but make sure the television screen is a reasonable size, or you may need two sets (and an adapter for the video recorder).

Many of the videos suggested may be hired or bought from your local Christian bookshop, or if you have difficulty in obtaining them, they can be hired from: Christian Resources Project (CRP), 14 Lipson Road, Plymouth, Devon PL4 8PW (0752 224012). They have an extensive range, and a free catalogue avaliable on request.

Scripture Union videos may be bought or hired from Scripture Union Mail Order, 9–11 Clothier Road, Bristol BS4 5RL (0272 719709). A free catalogue is available.

Books

The Chocolate Teapot by David Lawrence (Scripture Union) is highly recommended reading for young people, so do encourage your group members to buy a copy! Perhaps you could have some on a 'sale or return' basis from your local Christian bookshop. All about coping as a Christian at school, it deals with some of the issues covered in this book and encourages readers to stay in shape when the heat is on. It's an excellent book and very funny. A simple review, with a few short extracts, will probably sell all your copies!

The Bible

Each issue is examined from a biblical point of view, and if your group members don't already do so, why not encourage them to read the Bible for themselves on a regular basis? Not any easy task, but with a copy of *One to One* Bible reading notes, produced by Scripture Union for 11–13s, it should seem less daunting! Contents include The Grumps (a regular cartoon feature), Prayabout …, It Bugs Me! Problem Page, Inside Info, Hard Questions, One to One Club, puzzles and sketchscripts and lots more! The zany style should appeal to your group members, but remember they will need a lot of encouragement to keep going. After all, do *you* find it easy?

Understanding 11–13s

To gain a better understanding of 11–13s we need to find out how they 'tick', although most of the time they don't even know themselves! If we are to work effectively with them, we need to see things from their point of view (not that we can ever be one of them, nor should we try to be). They are at that awkward stage of being neither children, nor adults, but they are people and they are valuable, and they long to be recognised as such!

11–13s are …

Although generalisations are always wrong, the characteristics that are bound to show in someone in your group can be listed. That may give important clues about how to relate to them.

This is a time of rapid growth, with girls generally ahead of boys. Be patient with those who seem uncoordinated or clumsy – and since growing is hard work, try not to accuse those who are tired of being lazy!

This is also a time of intellectual growth, especially into abstract thinking. Encourage group members to think things through – especially with the Bible. And keep it imaginative, remembering that young people like adventure and discovery.

The characteristics typical of social change at this age are often painful: the need to belong, the aspiration to be fully adult, the sensitive self-consciousness, the tendency to hero worship. Be gentle and caring!

This is also a time of fluctuating emotions, including the lows when young people feel no one understands them! So make a special effort to get to know, appreciate and understand your group members.

These years are also a time of spiritual growth, as young people question received ideas and seek a faith of their own. See below!

Spiritual development

11–13s are intellectual, emotional and physical and their Christian faith is part of their 'make-up', involving thinking, feeling, and doing. They will all be at very different stages spiritually, and the diagram below may help us to understand this better.

According to John Westerhoff (*Will Our Children Have Faith?*, published by Seabury Press, New York), faith development can be illustrated in the following way:

Experienced faith
where someone simply feels loved and accepted

Affiliative faith
where someone enjoys being 'one of the crowd' – that is, experiencing and learning

Searching faith
where someone begins to ask serious questions in search of their own faith in God

Owned faith
where someone accepts Jesus as their Lord

Conversion comes as the 'bridge' between searching faith and owned faith. 'Conversion experiences may be sudden or gradual, dramatic or undramatic, emotional or intellectual, but they always involve a major change in a person's thinking, feeling and willing – in short, in their total behaviour' (John Westerhoff).

Many of your group members will be at the first stage, of experienced faith, which might then lead into affiliative faith. You may never see them reach the point of conversion as such, but you can be sure that your contact with them will be used by God. Who knows what might happen as they grow up? It may be years before they reach the stages of searching faith and owned faith. Your role is to encourage them, pray for them and leave them in God's hands.

Two of the most important things you can do for your group members are value them and pray for them. Before you can do that, you need to get to know them! Remembering their names is an obvious first step. Make a point of *learning* them, so that you don't make mistakes. As far as a group member is concerned, a leader who can't even remember what they are called doesn't rate very highly in their estimation. What about birthdays? Note the dates in your diary and send cards. It may seem a little thing, but it can mean such a lot. This is assuming you know where your group members live, of course.

Make it your business to find out about your group members' hobbies and interests. Have you ever thought of watching some of the television programmes they're into? Which secular magazines do they read? Why not get a few copies to keep you in touch with their world? Be aware of their home situations too. It's always helpful to know a little about the group members' families and it will prevent you putting your foot in it if, for example, there's only one parent at home, and not two. Above all, don't try too hard! Be natural and be yourself. You can't be one of them, but you can offer sincere friendship across the age gap.

11–13s have the same problem that we all have, except they can find it a lot more painful – that is, they don't feel very important. They're no longer children and some of the things they used to get excited about they now find silly. They are also at the bottom of the pile in a big secondary school, trying to come to terms with a body that is unpredictable, to say the least! No wonder they are sometimes loud, or bolshy. Well, how would you hide your insecurity? As their group leader, you can help them to feel valuable … Most things that happen to an 11–13 year old either give them a sense of value, or a sense of worthlessness.

A sense of value can be created by …
- being treated as an adult.
- being listened to.
- being complemented for their appearance.
- belonging and being accepted.
- being able to do what they're good at.
- being able to meet reasonable expectations.
- being given responsibility.
- having friends.

A sense of worthlessness can come from …
- being told that they're stupid when attempting to be adult.
- being unheard.
- feeling unattractive.
- feeling 'out of it'.
- having to live up to other people's expectations.
- being reminded of a bad past record.
- not being trusted.
- being lonely.

This introduction is the count-down: you're on the launchpad and your journey begins on the next page …

Introduction

This material aims to show group members that they can all do *something* – everyone has gifts of some sort. As well as helping each group member to recognise that they *do* have talents, and to discover what those talents are, the activities show the group members how to develop those gifts as God intended, so that they can be used individually, or for the benefit of the whole group. There is a questionnaire, several games, a short talk outline, a wordsearch and a sketchscript, as well as a 'Bible focus' activity to explore what the Bible says about the abilities God has given us. Your group members are at an age when their self-esteem is very fragile. This could be a valuable way of building up their confidence in themselves.

Icebreaker (10 minutes)

You will need: photocopies of the 'Talent spotter' sheets and pens – enough for all the group members to have one.

Explain to the group that the aim is to get as many different autographs as possible for each talent. Some people may be able to sign up for more than one thing!

Hand out a 'Talent spotter' sheet and pen to each member of the group. Ask group members to go around the room finding different people to sign beside the talents/gifts. Give them a time limit of, say, five minutes. You could have a kitchen pinger ticking in the background, which will ring loudly when the time is up!

Follow-up discussion questions:
- Are you a talented person? Be honest! (Maybe ask for a show of hands.)
- Did everyone sign something? *(All* hands should have been raised in that case!)
- So does that mean everyone is talented? (Everyone can do *something*!)
- Did anyone sign some of the really unusual abilities? (If so, what were they?)
- If we have gifts that weren't mentioned on the list, how can we find out what they are? (Ask people who know us well, such as parents, teachers, friends.)

Activity (5 minutes)

You will need: enough pencils and paper for all the group members.

Ask the group members to write down the gifts they think they have (honestly!) and then to jot down how they are going to use and/or develop them. If appropriate they could then get together with two or three other people who know

them quite well and each share what they have written, seeing if the others agree or disagree with what they think (If they are stuck and finding it difficult to identify their gifts, you could refer them back to the 'Talent spotter' sheet.) You will need to be careful that this activity doesn't become exclusive so that the shy, quieter members of the group are left out. Finish by reading 1 Peter 4:10–11.

Game (12 minutes)

You will need: sticky labels (enough for one for each person at least) pre-written with talents (use those from the 'Talent spotter' list or make up your own).

Aim: to re-emphasise the idea that talents/abilities do not need to be mega-human, they can be as simple as the ability to smile or to listen.

Divide the group into twos (or threes). Place a label on each person's back and explain that they have a talent written on them.

The talents may only be communicated through mime, so to discover their own talent they should watch the other person mime and then ask the question 'Am I good at …?' The mimer may only nod or shake their head in reply. Then they mime the other person's talent. When they have both (all) discovered their talent they should sit down.

If you have time, ask one or two pairs to mime their own talents and ask the others to identify them.

Explain that sometimes it's difficult for us to identify our own talents but with a little help from our friends we can begin to see where our talents lie. Talents don't need to be mega-big. It is far better to have a group of people who have small talents than one person who can do everything.

Talk outline (5 minutes)

'How do you feel when your friend gets much nicer birthday presents than you do? Are you happy for them, or do you sulk because yours weren't so good? Sometimes we have similar reactions when we look at the particular gifts which God has given us and we compare them with the ones he has given other people.' (Produce an easy jigsaw puzzle with about thirty pieces on it, having secretly already removed five or six pieces. Ask the group to try and put the puzzle together – they will discover that some of the bits are missing!) '*All* the parts are necessary to complete a jigsaw puzzle. (And it's very frustrating when they aren't all where they should be!) Not only is each part vital, each part is different, and it needs to be! Some are large, some small and they're all different shapes. A bit like us really!' (Finish by reading Romans 12:4–8 substituting the word 'jigsaw' for 'body'!)

Talent spotter

Get the autograph of someone in the group who ...

has climbed a mountain	goes jogging
plays the piano	is good with animals
enjoys cooking	can sing in tune
gets on well with children	enjoys acting
is organised	is a qualified life-saver
can swim	is easy to talk to
has a first aid certificate	is good with numbers
is neat and tidy!	is a good listener
is artistic	makes you laugh
enjoys sport	always has time for other people
is good with their hands	is good at speaking in public
is full of original ideas	is good with quiet or shy people
likes dancing	has a sense of rhythm
has a good memory	you would go to with a problem
is musical	reads a lot
likes talking to old people	is always smiling
doesn't mind the sight of blood	is good at following instructions

Videos

McGee and Me – Back to the Drawing Board A mixture of animation and live action produce an adventure story which helps viewers to apply biblical principles to everyday life. This story about a school poster competition deals with jealousy. (30 minutes – CRP)

The White Rock Blues Enzy is fed up with his job and tries all sorts of other things until he finds out what he does best. Cartoon parable about discovering our gifts. (10 minutes – CRP)

Profile of a Plastic Surgeon A Bristol plastic surgeon, at home and at work, talks about his job and how his faith helps him to cope with the pain and tragedy he sees every day. (23 minutes – CRP)

Project

Plan a panto, and give everyone in the group a job. Discuss how the team needed for a good production is made up of people who are very different, with different talents and abilities.

Suggestions for people needed:

- Director
- Producer
- Script writer
- Actors
- Costume makers
- Make up
- Props
- Front of house
- Lighting
- Stage management
- Prompt
- Understudies
- Musicians
- Singers
- Dancers
- Programme designers

If this idea really takes off, you could arrange to perform it at a local old peoples' home. It would be an excellent way to get your group working together!

Sketchscript: Our hero? (5 minutes)

Cast: narrator, new group member, five other group members, the group leader (as themselves!).

Props: a packet of felt pens, a football, a dustpan and brush, a guitar or guitar case, a 'comic-relief' style red nose.

(This will need careful, supervised rehearsal – a good way for the cast to put their various gifts and talents into practice! The final presentation should be slick and fast-moving, with clear miming.)

NARRATOR: Meet our new member. *(Enter new member, waving and smiling.)*

NARRATOR: Whose group expect him to … *(Five group members come on stage in turn and one at a time hand the new member a prop. He looks at each one doubtfully, but they insist, and press it on him. When he is offered the clown's red nose, he smiles and puts it on very happily. After they have loaded him with their props the other group members move back and stand in line, drumming their fingers and watching expectantly.)*

NARRATOR: He tries *(New group member tries to sweep the floor and kick the football etc.)*

NARRATOR: … and struggles *(New group member really struggles to try and do everything.)*

NARRATOR: … but it's all too much. *(New group member drops everything and shrugs his shoulders as if to say, 'I can't cope. I give up!')*

NARRATOR: To the rescue! *(Enter the real group leader who mops the new member's brow, and picks everything up.)*

NARRATOR: There must be a better way! *(Group leader suddenly notices other group members in line and one at a time, hands objects to them which they consider carefully, before accepting with a nod and a smile as if to say, 'Yes, I can do that!' When it comes to the red nose, the new member is reluctant to part with it and indicates that he would like to keep it as it is his 'gift'. The group leader nods and then takes the dustpan from the other group member who has been given the dustpan and brush and gives it to the last group member. Those two other group members nod and smile at each other as if to say, 'We can share these and do the job together').*

NARRATOR: There is a better way! We all need each other! *(The cast all join hands and take a bow.)*

Activity (15 minutes)

Divide the group into small groups. Ask the groups if they have discovered what their particular gifts are and, if so what they are going to do about them. Ask the small groups to show how our gifts need to be practised and used by composing a play or short story about a piano player who never practised, or a sportsman who never did any training (or a similar scenario which they can invent themselves). Give a time limit of, say, ten minutes and then get the groups to perform their plays or read their stories to the rest of the group. (If a group chooses to write a story, they may need paper and pencils.)

Visiting speakers

Perhaps you could arrange for someone local (an artist, a nurse, a musician …) to visit the group and talk to them about their particular gift or skill, how they developed it and how they are using it now.

Bible focus (15 minutes)

There are different abilities to perform service, but the same God gives ability to all for their particular service (1 Corinthians 12:6).

You will need: Bibles, pens, paper, a large sheet of paper or overhead projector acetate, 'Gifts galore' sheets, (enough for one per group member) and some pre-wrapped 'presents' – at least as many as there are group members.

Hand out the Bibles, pens and sheets. Read 1 Corinthians 12:8–11 and ask group members to fill in the boxes on the sheet to show the gifts of the Spirit mentioned in the reading. (You may need to help them.)

If it's appropriate for your group, you could also draw attention to the other gifts mentioned in the Bible. There are two more 'lists' in Romans 12:6–8 and Ephesians 4:11–12. (You could make a list of all the gifts mentioned in the three passages.)

Ask the group to think about the people in their group. What are they good at? Hand out the paper and together make a list of abilities represented in your group. Do it individually to start with, then collate the ideas on a large sheet of paper or overhead projector acetate. Try to think of at least one gift for each member of the group.

Have ready the gift-wrapped boxes of various sizes. Write each ability from the group's list onto a box, then give the boxes out. Each person should receive a box, some more than one. Some boxes are large; others are small.

Point out that abilities, like birthday presents, should not be left unwrapped and unused, they should be opened and used to give pleasure not only to the person who received them, but pleasure to the person who gave them. (Perhaps your boxes could contain a few sweets as an unexpected bonus! To make the point, the sweets could be shared …)

Talk about how God has given each of us a 'gift' of something special and individual. Are we willing to 'open' it for him? For example, if we are good at singing, how could we use that for God?

Moses didn't think he was any good. Read together Exodus 3:11,13, 4:1, 4:10,13 to see how God gave him the ability to do what he was asked.

Finish with this prayer:

Thank you, Father, for the gifts you have given to me.
Help me to use them. Help me not to hide them away. Amen.

```
T E L K Q U I H L R P H T S P
N A L C T E G L U A G A E T R
E S H B M U S I C A L T A A O
I L E Y A R P M Q K M L C S P
T S A L R E A S I N G Q H T H
A R R I G H G X L U U A R N E
P M S C T S R D Q I E E Y E S
C Q N H U M B L E P S I E T Y
D A N C E I E T O L I S S S Q
P Z R A T L T L O B W E I I U
R Q U E S E S V S M L O O L I
L A G R L A E H C O R P N S T
L M H P Q R A B R I G H T K E
```

Gifts galore!

In 1 Corinthians 12:8–11 you will find a list of the special 'gifts of the Spirit' which are for use in the church. Can you complete the labels on these nine gifts?

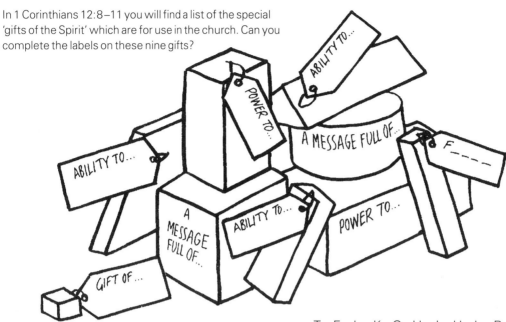

Find these abilities in the grid on the right.

smile	preach
listen	teach
laugh	prophesy
talk	heal
sing	pray
dance	wise
care	bright
love	musical
patient	knowledgeable
humble	quiet

Which of these are you good at?

```
T E L K Q U I H L R P H T S P
N A L C T E G L U A G A E T R
E S H B M U S I C A L T A A O
I L E Y A R P M Q K M L C S P
T S A L R E A S I N G Q H T H
A R R I G H G X L U U A R N E
P M S C T S R D Q I E E Y E S
C Q N H U M B L E P S I E T Y
D A N C E I E T O L I S S S Q
P Z R A T L T L O B W E I I U
R Q U E S E S V S M L O O L I
L A G R L A E H C O R P N S T
L M H P Q R A B R I G H T K E
```

Cartoon

Try to draw a cartoon to show each of the abilities mentioned in the wordsearch. Here are three to get you started.

Someone oozing love   Someone who is wise

Or maybe draw someone who has more than one talent

A good listener
who is also musical!

2. Bad habits

Introduction

Icebreakers, a short story, role-play scenarios and discussion questions help a group to get to grips with some of the pressures to conform which they face at school, and with their friends. 'Bad habits' deals with alcohol and solvent abuse, drugs, gossip and bad language. You may well find that once this subject has been broached, and the group members realise that you are not easily shocked, and very willing to talk about these issues honestly, they will discuss some of the problems they face very frankly. Remember, too, that they need your prayers as they cope with the hostile environment of today's world. The aim is to avoid being overly legalistic or negative, but the subject matter demands that sometimes. However, the pressure to be 'one of the crowd' is so strong that some of the material dealing with self-image in other chapters may be appropriate to use with this topic. As the young people realise that they are valued by God and build up their own self-esteem, it may give them the confidence and courage they need to stand up for what they believe to be right and not be afraid of being different. In particular, the talk outline, sketchscripts and 'Reflections' funsheet from the chapter on 'Failure', and the icebreaker from the chapter on 'Hassle' may be relevant.

Icebreakers (5 minutes each)

1. Play the 'Yes and No' game. Ask for a volunteer and explain that you are going to ask some questions and that they must answer without using the words 'Yes' or 'No'. Fire the questions thick and fast and see if the contestant can keep the rules for one minute. (Examples of questions: Are you a boy/girl? Is your name …? Do you like chocolate? Are you tall?)

    Alternatively choose some other prohibition, such as they must not use any words starting with T in their answers. (You could divide the group into pairs and get everyone playing at once.)

2. Ask for three or four volunteers and give each a sugar-coated doughnut which they must eat without licking their lips. Anyone licking is out! Get the non-participating group members to judge – they will anyway!

Point out how, in both of the above games, it is hard to break the habit of either (a) using the words Yes or No when answering or (b) licking your lips when eating doughnuts. (Both can be done, so be warned!) This introduces the idea of 'automatically doing things without thinking' or even 'automatically doing or saying things that we know we shouldn't' – ie bad habits.

Story (3 minutes)

King Arthur and the Short Knight

King Arthur and certain of his knights were making their yearly pilgrimage to Glastonbury. Passing through the Enchanted Forest they came in sight of a richly coloured tent. Standing beside it, dressed all in bright armour, stood a tiny knight no more than two feet tall. As the party approached he stepped forward, barring the way.

'How now!' cried Arthur in mocking tone, 'May no one pass this way without a fight?'

'That is so!' answered the knight in a bold but squeaky voice. 'Are you ready?'

King Arthur and his men laughed heartily at this, and paying the knight no more attention than if he had been a sprig of bramble, rode past him and continued on their way.

The next year, at the same time and in the same place, the party came once more upon the tent and the knight, who appeared to have grown somewhat in stature, being now some four feet tall. As before he issued his challenge, and as before King Arthur refused to fight him and rode haughtily past.

The next year the small knight was the size of a strong youth, but still King Arthur would not fight him. But in the fourth year, when they reached the tent in the Enchanted Forest, the knight was nowhere to be seen … They had not gone ten yards further when their way was suddenly blocked by a knight of gigantic proportions who wielded a mighty two-handed sword.

'You must fight me now!' said he in a voice of thunder.

Arthur dismounted and with shield and sword King and knight sprang towards each other to do battle: a great crash rang through the forest as they met. Again and again they struck at one another, but at last the stronger knight began to gain the upper hand. Quite suddenly the knight drew back, and Arthur, thinking him to be exhausted, leapt towards him. With remarkable speed the Knight swung the great sword above his head and brought it down with all his might against the King's shield. Such power was in that blow that Arthur was sent reeling to the ground. Looking up he saw the knight standing over him in triumph, and felt the point of his huge sword against his throat.

'I do not ask for mercy,' said Arthur, 'for had I accepted your challenge earlier, as I should have done, I would not now find myself in this estate. But tell me one thing, strange knight: what is your name?'

'My name …' said the giant with a little smile '… is Bad Habit!'

Activity (3 minutes)

You will need: an overhead projector or a large sheet of paper and different coloured pens.

Have a quick brainstorm on definitions of the word 'habit'. Refer to the list below if necessary and write all the definitions on the sheet. A habit is:
- A tendency to act in a particular way.
- Established custom, usual practice.
- A learned response to a particular situation.
- An addiction to a particular substance (such as nicotine or solvents).

Ask the group to give examples of each definition, if they can, and then ask if anyone would like to share with the group what their habits are! (Examples could include nail-biting or thumb-sucking!) Be prepared to divulge *your* habits!

Explain that for a Christian, a 'bad' habit could be defined as: 'a tendency to act in a way that God disapproves of'.

Write this on the sheet and refer back to the list of habits. Which ones are harm*less* and which ones harm*ful* and the sort of 'bad' habit to be avoided? Why?

Activity (8 minutes)

You will need: several newspapers (tabloid rather than the *Financial Times*!!) and thick black felt pens. (You may want to remove page 3 from certain papers …)

Ask the group to imagine what difference it would make to life if all of the 'bad habits' were to disappear from the face of the earth and all that was left were the good ones! Newspapers would have nothing left to report!

Divide the group into twos and threes and give each small group a newspaper and a pen. Ask them to black out all the passages reporting peoples' 'bad habits' censor-style. After two or three minutes report back on the results – they will probably find they are not left with much news at the end of the exercise!

To conclude this exercise, read Romans 6:12–14, substituting the words 'bad habits' for the word 'sin'. The Bible offers hope: our bad habits can be replaced with a new way of living – God's way.

Bible focus (12 minutes)

You will need: an instruction manual for a complicated, expensive piece of equipment (such as computer or video recorder), Bibles for everyone, three or more pens, and an overhead projector acetate or large sheet of paper with the following chart drawn on it in advance.

Introduce this Bible focus by explaining that if we had a new computer or video recorder (or whatever) we would make sure that we knew how to use it properly. How would we do that? (Show the group the instruction manual.) In the same way, we are intricately made by God with an instruction manual for the best way to live! (Show the group a Bible.) This manual points out things to avoid (bad habits) and things to aim for (good habits). Divide the group into three smaller

Bad habits	Good habits
What action can we take? How can we change?	

groups and then display the chart for them all to see. Give each group a list of Bible verses to find and a pen and ask them to write any key words from each passage in their section of the chart. Explain that if something is already on the list, and it appears in another reference, they don't need to add it to the chart – once is enough!
- **Group 1 – Bad habits:** Colossians 3:5–10; Galatians 5:19–21; Ephesians 5:3–5; Proverbs 6:16–19.
- **Group 2 – Good habits:** Galatians 5: 22–23; Romans 12:9–21; Colossians 3:12–17; Ephesians 4:22–32.
- **Group 3 – Action:** Romans 12: 2; Galatians 5: 25; Proverbs 3: 5–7; Proverbs 4:14–15, 23–24.

After about eight minutes, conclude by referring to the chart and the action necessary.

Prayer idea (7 minutes)

It may be that some of the young people really are ashamed of their bad habits and need a chance to respond. Sing, play or read 'River wash over me' (*Mission Praise* 548) together. Emphasise the three elements of: our confession, God's cleansing and our invitation to Jesus to be Lord of our habits.

Discussion (15–20 minutes)

You will need to judge your particular group before attempting these discussion questions. Bear in mind that there are no easy answers, and life at school will put your group members under pressure to experiment with solvents, cigarettes or alcohol. If you feel out of your depth, maybe you could invite a suitable visitor (Christian youth worker, social worker or doctor) to lead the discussion, or even give a short talk and answer questions.

1. How do people who are drunk often behave? (Slurred speech, lack of co-ordination, loss of balance, talkative, aggressive, violent.) These things can be amusing, but how can people under the influence of alcohol be a danger to themselves or others?
2. Read Proverbs 23:29–35. What does the Bible say about drinking too much? What do you think a sensible attitude to drink should be?

3. What sorts of addictive habits do some people at your school indulge in? (Glue-sniffing, smoking, drinking, taking drugs.) Why do you think they do it? (To be 'one of the crowd', because they'll get laughed at if they don't, because it's exciting.) Do you think the fun and excitement some of these things give, lasts? Do you think the people who do these things are really happy?

4. If you haven't already been offered cigarettes, drugs, or the chance to sniff glue, you probably will be at some stage. Do you know what you would do or say? Would having a 'ready answer' help? If so, what sort of thing could you say, if you wanted to refuse?

5. Which bad habits would you say were simply anti-social (burping, picking your nose etc), which harmful (drinking too much, smoking, taking drugs etc), and which unbiblical (blaspheming, gossiping etc)?

Who would we please by giving up each sort of habit?

Talk outline (5 minutes)

As far as our habits are concerned, we all make excuses and say things like, 'I can't help myself', or, 'It's just the way I am.' If we want to do something about a particular habit, we will never shake it off until we take responsibility for it. On the whole, we choose to do it. People who use bad language at school usually manage not to at home, for example, which proves that it's a thing they can control if they have to.

Sometimes we make excuses and use 'nice' words to make our bad habits seem more acceptable. We may say, 'Everyone does it!' or perhaps we call lies 'fibs' or 'half-truths'. But the Bible has an uncomfortable name for the wrong things which creep into our lives and sometimes stay there – sin. God hates sin, and anyone who wants to follow God's way and please him, will want to get rid of those things. Although God hates sin, he loves the 'sinner' and forgives them.

For a Christian, then, the first step to getting rid of a bad habit is to tell God about it and ask for his forgiveness. Habits won't disappear overnight, but if we really mean business, we will be able to overcome them eventually if we don't give up. Having a practical plan to put into operation when necessary might help! Here are some suggestions:

- Don't get discouraged if you slip back into your habit sometimes. After all, if it's a habit it will take time to shift! Don't give up! Use your mistake to remind you to be on your guard in future.
- If you have a particular weakness such as bad language (you can't stop using it), or dirty jokes (you enjoy telling them or listening to them), make a conscious effort to avoid situations where you come across them. It will be *very* difficult to do, but if you really want to overcome those habits it will need drastic action. It may mean not spending so much time with certain people or even not watching particular programmes on television. Why not treat yourself to some sort of 'reward' each time you manage to overcome your habit?

- Perhaps you could find a close friend and draw up a 'contract' together. This will involve helping each other to overcome particular habits, so you'll need to be really honest with each other. If there are several bad habits you need to deal with, start with just one thing. Get your friend to check up on you and you do the same for them. Knowing someone else is watching you might help! In advance, work out something else you could both do when you find yourself about to slip into your habit, and do it instead if you can. Even using some sort of 'code-word' to remind each other to be on guard may help!
- If you decide to put a certain amount of money in a tin every time you slip back into your bad habit, you may find it helps you to overcome it quite quickly! The money collected could then be sent to charity!

Role play (15 minutes)

The habitual liar

Divide the group into threes and fours and ask them to use the mini-scenarios given below to create a short sketch. Each sketch should have two endings as indicated. When the groups are ready, watch a few performances and discuss the problems/merits of telling the truth in all circumstances.

Scenario 1 A friend asks you what you think of his/her new hairstyle which doesn't suit him/her at all. Develop the scene with two endings:
a. Tell the truth about your opinions.
b. Make up an answer that you think your friend wants to hear!

Scenario 2 You watched TV rather than do your French homework, thinking that you'd be able to copy it from your friend when you got to school. When you arrive at school your friend is off sick. How do you explain the non-appearance of your homework to your French teacher? Make up two endings:
a. Invent a good excuse as to why it's not done.
b. Own up and face the consequences.

Scenario 3 Your friends start talking quite spitefully about another person in your class. You know that many of the things that they are saying are not true. Make two endings to your sketch:
a. Join in with your friends so that they accept you.
b. Stand up for the innocent person and tell the truth about them.

Videos

Caught in Time Two American schoolboys crash their motorbike after a party and find themselves in first century Palestine. They meet Jesus and are challenged about their twentieth century lifestyle. (55 minutes – CRP)

McGee and Me – The Big Lie Eleven year old Nicholas has a cartoon character friend called McGee, whose advice is not always reliable. In this episode, Nicholas discovers that telling lies is not a convenient way to make friends. (30 minutes – CRP)

3. Death

Introduction

Death (like sex in Victorian times) is often a taboo subject. This material aims to dismiss some of the 'mystique' which surrounds death and look at what happens when people die, what Christians believe and how we can cope with death, whether losing a loved one or facing up to the prospect of our own death one day. It's the 'unknown' which can make death so frightening and so we suggest that you invite a guest panel for the group members to question frankly, to include a doctor, a vicar, someone who works in a hospice and possibly even an undertaker! Obviously this whole subject needs to be dealt with very sensitively – make sure you are aware of any bereavements your group members may have suffered recently.

Icebreaker (5 minutes)

Without comment on the theme, introduce the following quick quiz and ask the group members to guess what the theme is. (It shouldn't be too difficult!)
1. Who chopped his wives heads off for a hobby? (Henry VIII)
2. Which member of the Beatles was shot in New York? (John Lennon)
3. What is a mortuary? (Building where dead bodies are kept)
4. A Russian statesman's body was embalmed and put on display after his death. Can you name him? (Lenin)
5. What is another name for a dead body beginning with C? (Cadaver or corpse)
6. What is a coroner's job?(Investigating the cause of death in a court)
7. What does an undertaker do for a living? (Arranges funerals)
8. What is a coffin usually made of? (Wood)
9. What is murder? (Unlawful killing of a human being)
10. How did Jesus die? (He was crucified)

Discussion (10 minutes)

It may be appropriate with your particular group to assess what experience, if any, they have had of death. It may be limited to what they see on television or films, or read in the papers or in books. For some, though, it may be that they have lost friends or relatives. The group may also want to mention pets who have died. Ask who has any experience of death, and you will probably find that they are more than willing to talk! Encourage them to be sensitive to each other and to listen to each other. If they are reticent, you could ask them if they know of any famous people who have died recently, or if they have recently seen reports of death on the news.

Activity (5 minutes)

You will need: a small slip of paper and a pencil for everyone, and a container.

Ask the group to jot down one or two words on their slip of paper to describe their feelings about death (such as fear, anxiety, worry etc). Put them all in a container and then remove them one at a time and read them out anonymously. You could write them on an overhead projector acetate or large sheet of paper.

Bible focus (10 minutes)

Christians believe that people who have asked God to be in control of their lives will be with him in heaven one day. Their earthly bodies will die, but their spirits will live. This is difficult to understand, so to help them, divide the group into seven smaller groups to look at the Bible. Ask each of the small groups to read the Bible verses and try and answer the question relating to those verses. It may be helpful to have the questions written on an overhead projector acetate or a large sheet of paper. In turn the small groups can choose a person to read out both the verses and their answer. The answers could then be written in as you go along (in a different coloured pen to make them clear!).
1. Romans 5:12. Why did death come into the world? (Because of sin)
2. Romans 6:9–11. Who has power over sin? (Jesus)
3. Romans 6:23. What is God's gift to us? (Eternal life)
4. Romans 8:38–39. Death can't separate us from what? (God's love)
5. John 11:25. If we believe in Jesus, what will happen after we die? (We will live)
6. 2 Corinthians 5:1. What are our bodies likened to? (A tent)
7. John 14:1–2. Who is preparing a place for us in heaven? (God)

Visiting speakers

A visit from a Christian doctor, the local vicar or minister, someone who works in a hospice, an undertaker or someone who works in a crematorium could be very helpful, especially if you have the sort of group that don't mind asking questions! You could ask a group of visitors to form a 'panel' or invite one person to give a short talk about their work . You could invite several speakers over a period of a few weeks. They would probably be pleased to have the opportunity to talk to the group, if perhaps a little surprised to be asked! Such people talking about their involvement with death would help to allay fears and remove some of the 'mystique' surrounding the whole subject. As far as the group's questions are concerned, it might be a good idea to have a few prepared beforehand to get the ball rolling! On the whole, people in these professions are not easily shocked, so don't be afraid to let the group ask the questions that they want to ask! You could ask:

- Why did you decide to go into your particular job?
- Doesn't it make you depressed, dealing with people who are dying or have died?
- What happens to someone's body after they have died?
- Why are some people buried and some people cremated? Does it matter which happens?
- How do you help the relatives and friends of the person who is dying or has died?

You could also ask the vicar or minister to visit on a separate occasion to go through the funeral service and explain it to the group. Also, if you know anyone suitable (and know them well enough), ask someone who has been bereaved for a while to visit the group and share how they cope with their loss, although you would have to make sure that your group would be sensitive to this person.

Do make sure that someone from the group writes to thank the speakers for their visit.

Activity (3 minutes)

Explain that you have one or two 'problem page' letters plus answers and then read them yourself or get group members to read them out.

If God gives us life, why do people die?

When God made the world, it wasn't part of his plan for people to die. Death is ugly and unnatural. God told the first people they would die if they disobeyed his command. They chose to ignore what he said. And so death came into the world. But even then God had planned a way for people to live. He sent Jesus to offer people 'eternal life' as his gift. For all who accept his gift, death is not the end. It's just the gateway to a new life with him.

What happens to you when you die?

Think what happens when you move house. You leave the building behind and take with you all that matters from inside it. Your body is like a house containing all the important things inside it. When we die, we leave our old bodies behind because they are now of no use to us. And we take what's really important, the real you and me, with us. Just as snakes shed their old skins, so we shed our old bodies when we die and our real selves go to heaven.

Sketchscript: The controller (3 minutes)

Cast: Death, the puppeteer **D**; boy puppet **B**; girl puppet **G**; Jesus (an adult) **J**.

Props:

- (for the puppeteer) dark glasses, a black hat with the word DEATH stuck on it, a dark suit or cape, two puppet controls made from white pieces of wood nailed across each other at the centre point;
- (for the puppets, one girl and one boy) costumes that make them look like puppets, rosy cheeks and red noses. To each of their hands and feet is attached a length of thick, white elastic – one end is nailed to the puppeteer's controls, the other is tied around the hands and feet;
- (for Jesus, who should be played by an adult) a large sharp knife with a crosspiece put on it to make it look like a cross, and a colourful 'J' stuck on to a T-shirt.

The idea of this sketch is to show that even though everyone has to die and it looks as if death is in control, Jesus has the power to set people free so that death isn't the end for them. The sketch is very short and simple, but, for it to be really effective, you'll need to spend a long time rehearsing and getting the costumes and props together.

The scene opens with the two puppets flopped lifelessly together in front of a chair. Their strings and controls are draped over the chair – but make sure they don't get tangled up!

DEATH enters. He is the arch-villain and has a wicked laugh. He rubs his hands with glee and cackles when he sees **B** and **G**. He picks up the two puppet controls and climbs on to the chair. For the rest of the action, he needs to make it look as if he is controlling the puppets, though the elastic 'strings' are intended to make this a bit easier!

D raises **B** and **G** up from the floor exactly together – this needs a lot of rehearsal! First their heads are raised, then both arms, then bottoms etc, all in jerky movements. **B** and **G** must have silly grins on all the while and should try not to change the expressions on their faces at all.

When **B** and **G** are both on their feet, they go into a little synchronized dance routine that has been carefully worked out. All this time **D** looks at them gleefully. He should chuckle wickedly sometimes.

Then **B** and **G** mime exactly together the motion of life – eating, drinking, digging. **D** turns away slightly and has a laugh with the audience. At this point **J** enters holding the cross/knife so that it's clear what it is. Be careful – it's very sharp! He cuts **B**'s strings, but **B** carries on exactly as before. **J** exits. **D** hasn't noticed what has happened and carries on with both controls just the same.

B and **G** start to slow down and get old. They both die. **D** is double-extra-happy! He climbs down, puts both controls on the chair and throws **G** over his shoulder. He cackles to **B** – 'I'll be back for you in just a tick!' **D** turns away from **B** and carries **G** off. But **B** starts to get up – he has a new life of his own. **D** notices and is horrified. He grabs for **B** but **B** dances off in a puppet-like way. He's free! **D** lets out a cry of despair and holds his hand out in a grasp towards the direction **B** has disappeared off. Freeze.

Outside visit

Perhaps you could arrange with your local vicar or minister for members of your group who wanted to, to visit someone who is lonely (and, possibly, bereaved). Older people in particular love visits, especially from youngsters, and the group members could maybe commit themselves to, say, fortnightly visits after school for half an hour or so. On the whole they will only need to be prepared to listen, but occasionally they may be required to do a little shopping or walk a dog ... This kind of scheme needs to be set up *very* carefully and with long-term commitment, making sure that visitors are properly 'vetted' and that parents are happy to allow their son or daughter to take part in the scheme.

What's heaven like?

Dying is like going into the unknown – sort of! But it's not the end. Christians are going to be with God in heaven.

What will we do there? Rev 7:15

Who'll be there? Rev 7:9

Who will we worship? Rev 7:10,12

How will we feel? Rev 7:16,17

What will we always be aware of? Rev 21:3

Who will there **not** be? Rev 21:4

Who will look after us? Rev 21:7

But what does it **look** like?

The apostle John tried to describe the indescribable. Read Rev 21:10 – 22:5 and let your imagination run wild as you imagine yourself living there with God – forever!

Bible focus (10 minutes)

The 'What's heaven like?' sheet gives a Bible focus which you could do in small groups or which group members could do at home.

Activity (15 minutes)

You will need: obituaries, a dictionary, enough 'Here lies' sheets for one per person, and some pencils.

Ask the group if they know what an obituary or epitaph is, and if they don't, either explain to them, or hand out a dictionary and get some of the group members to look up the words and read out the definitions! Read out some extracts from two or three recent obituaries in the newspapers. (It doesn't matter if no one has never heard of the person concerned – it's the content which matters!) Ask the group: What kinds of things do people tend to say? Why would it have been a good idea to say some of those things before the person had died?

Ask the group how they feel about writing their own epitaph! Hand out the sheets and pencils and give them a few hints if necessary. (What, for example, would they like people to remember them for? Have they any particular skills they would like to mention? What about their personality? Have they any burning ambitions they want to fulfil which they could presume they had already achieved, and mention?)

Suggest to the group that they do something positive about appreciating other people while they are still alive! Get them to compose a letter on the back of their sheets to someone who is special to them, perhaps a close friend or relative. It doesn't need to be an epistle – just a few words telling that person how much they are appreciated, perhaps for the way they do something, or the type of personality they have. Or, if the group members aren't struck on that idea, how about asking them to send someone special a 'non-Valentine's day card'? Those who do write a letter could transfer their message to a card or letter at home, and actually send it to the person concerned.

Activity (10 minutes)

Using an overhead projector or large sheet of paper have a brainstorm with the group on the feelings experienced when a loved one dies. (Be sensitive to any group members who may have been bereaved recently.) If the group is reticent, write up one or two of the following words to get them started: Shock, disbelief, anger, sadness, tears, anguish, desolation, pain, mourning, loneliness, sorrow, guilt, regret, bitterness, acceptance …

Explain that all these feeling are quite normal and someone who has been bereaved may experience all or some of them over a period of time. Christians feel the same way, even though they know that their loved one is with God. 'Mourning' in some cultures follows a carefully controlled and often lengthy process, which aims to help the bereaved person let their grief and sorrow out. Often people wear black clothes as a sign that they are mourning the loss of a loved one. The funeral service can be very helpful for those

left behind. It is a chance to be thankful for the person's life, to remember the happy times and to say 'Goodbye', with friends and relatives there to give support and comfort. If appropriate, you could read one or two extracts from the funeral service at this point.

Meditation (2 minutes)

Since I met you, I'm not afraid
(Found on the body of a soldier, killed in action in Vietnam)

> Look, God, I have never spoken to you,
> But now I want to say, 'How do you do?'
> You see, God, they told me you didn't exist
> And, like a fool, I believed all this.
>
> Last night from a shell hole, I saw your sky,
> I figured right then they had told me a lie,
> Had I taken time to see things you made,
> I'd known they weren't calling a spade, a spade.
>
> I wonder God if you'd shake my hand,
> Somehow I feel that You'll understand.
> Funny I had to come to this hellish place
> Before I had time to see your face.
>
> Well I guess there isn't much to say
> But I'm sure glad God, that I met you today.
> I guess the 'zero' hour will soon be here,
> But I'm not afraid since I know you're near.
>
> The signal! Well, God, I'll have to go,
> I like you lots, this I want you to know.
> Look now, this will be a horrible fight,
> Who knows, I may come to your house tonight.
>
> Though I wasn't friendly to you before,
> I wonder God, if you'd wait at your door,
> Look! I'm crying! Me! Shedding tears!
> I wish I'd known you these many years.
>
> Well, I have to go now, God, good-bye.
> Strange, since I met you,
> I'm not afraid to die.

Videos

Rich Man, Poor Man 'At twelve o'clock tonight the richest man in Silica Dale will die.' Faced with the prospect of his imminent death, Bigsby is fearful and panic-stricken. The nail-biting countdown begins … (15 minutes – CRP/Scripture Union)

Good Friday/Easter Sunday A sensitive and moving re-telling of the events of Jesus' death and resurrection, taken from the gospel accounts. Narrated by Fulton Mackay. (10 minutes x 2 – CRP/Scripture Union)

The Hitch Hiker's Guide to Eternity. Guide 1, Part 2: Death The staff at the Guide's editorial office are under pressure to sort out some burning issues before the boss comes back. (20 minutes – CRP)

Jill A sensitive documentary about a young Christian girl with cancer who has only a few months to live. (27 minutes – CRP)

To the memory of

Emma & Maria

LITTLEBOY

the twin children of
George and Emma Littleboy
of Hornsey
who died July 16th 1837

*two littleboys lie here
yet strange to say
these littleboys are girls*

In Memory of

Mrs Phoebe Crewe

who died May 28, 1817
aged 77 yrs

who, during 40 years as a
Midwife in this City brought into the
world 9730 children

How would you like to be remembered?
Write your own epitaph.

4. Evil

Introduction

This is a difficult subject to tackle! You will have to steer a course between two extremes: first, playing upon the (natural) fascination which young people have with the occult and supernatural, so that you arouse an unhealthy interest and perhaps do more harm than good: second, avoiding it to such an extent that your treatment becomes purely academic and philosophical. The subject of evil includes supernatural evil, and it would be wrong not to deal with it and give the kind of warnings which are necessary. But it's wider than that, too, and you should aim to communicate, above all, that evil is not glamorous or fascinating: that God's power is far greater than any other force in the universe: and that we have therefore nothing to be frightened of as long as he is with us. Good books which can help your own thinking are Nigel Wright's *The Fair Face of Evil* (Kingsway), Michael Green's *I Believe in Satan's Downfall* (Hodder) and Michael Perry's *Deliverance* (SPCK).

Because occult involvement can cause really big problems, you may find that this session unearths some serious personal and spiritual problems. Locate a trained counsellor experienced in these things *before* you run the session.

Icebreaker (15 minutes)

Break up the group into competing teams of three or four. Give them a pile of old newspapers each, three large sheets of paper, a pair of scissors and a glue stick. Tell them they have five minutes to cut out of the papers as many stories as possible in which something *evil* happens. (Wars, murders, famines, tragedies, robberies, etc, are bound to feature.)

Stop them after five minutes and ask them to look at each of the stories they've found, and decide *who is to blame* for the evil in each case. Give them five minutes more.

Then discuss your results. The responsibility is sometimes easy to assign: when something is stolen, the thief is responsible. But some evils are the result of natural disasters. Some seem to have no one individual who is responsible (who is to blame for the Third World debt problem, for example?). And with others – where an act of great, monstrous evil is committed – we might feel that although one person did it, he was possessed by a force stronger than himself.

Explain that the Bible says that 'evil' is a bigger problem than just human wrongdoing. (Nigel Wright: 'Humans are both the perpetrators of sin and its victims … By itself mankind is neither clever enough nor sufficiently demonic to be the originator of evil. We are tempted by a power that is beyond us and which pre-exists us.' Evil is a real force in the world: it accounts for the natural disasters which spoil God's creation, *and* is part of the atrocities and horrors which human beings inflict on each other. We need to know a bit about it to make a success of living on this planet.

Story (15 minutes)

Far away in the depths of the galaxy lie four identical planets. Orwok, Argor, Namek and Zykog. But living on each of the four is a very different experience.

Orwok is ruled by the wicked fiend Orbor. There is little joy on this planet. Happiness is strictly limited, and when good things happen, it is only so that Orbor can crush them immediately, destroying hope and spreading suffering.

Argor is a battlefield. The good forces of light are engaged in constant war against the grim forces of darkness, and week after week the tide of battle turns first one way, then another. No one can say who will eventually win. The warring armies are almost exactly matched.

Namek is ruled by a wise and just Planetary Controller who has a brilliantly conceived plan to make his planet a paradise. Yet he has his enemies, who constantly make trouble for his people, and try to spread the impression that they are truly in control. However, they are actually weak and scattered, and it is only a matter of time until they will be crushed decisively.

Zykog is an unpredictable planet where no one seems to be in charge. Most people do whatever seems right to them. Quite often bad people prosper and good people are punished, but nobody can work out what the laws are or who is enforcing them.

Ask the group which of these planets they would prefer to live on. Which of these planets sounds most like earth? Which of these planets comes closest to the Bible's picture of the way things are? Is evil more powerful than good; is good more powerful than evil; are both forces equally matched; or is there no sense in any of it?

Activity (15 minutes)

Divide the group into three teams. Give each team six cards, on which are written a selection of the following phrases:

- The serpent
- The enemy
- The ruler of this world
- The deceiver
- The prince of the power of the air
- The accuser
- The King of Hell
- The god of hell fire
- The spy
- The tormentor

Each team has to decide which of its cards are real biblical descriptions of the devil, and which aren't. (If you're in any doubt, the last four on the right are fakes! Ensure each team has four correct ones and two fakes.) They then have to try to trade the ones they have rejected with another group, so that they end up with six real ones. Stop the trading after a few minutes and see if any group has achieved this objective. Then talk about the significance of the true names, and what they tell us about the way evil operates.

Case studies (15 minutes)

Split into small groups (or stay together if there aren't many of you) and discuss these case studies together.

1. You read your horoscope in the paper. It says that you will have a sudden improvement in your financial circumstances, an unexpected shock and a meeting with an attractive new admirer. Later in the day you find 5 pence in the street, and as you bend down to pick it up you are nearly run over by a bus. But the admirer fails to appear. What do you think?
   a. This is all a load of rubbish.
   b. The stars never lie.
   c. Sometimes predictions come true, but just by chance.
   d. Sometimes predictions come true because an evil power may be at work behind the scenes.

2. The grandfather of a girl in your class has just died, three weeks ago. One night last week she woke up suddenly and thought she saw him standing at the end of her bed. What do you think?
   a. She was just being hysterical.
   b. It was the spirit of her grandfather.
   c. There is a natural explanation for this kind of thing.
   d. It was an evil spirit.

3. Some people you know at school have been playing with a ouija board. They claim it has answered all sorts of questions for them and told them things which were true, but which none of them knew before. What do you think?
   a. Ouija boards are faked. One of the people in the group was making the glass move by pushing it.
   b. Ouija boards are controlled by evil spirits.
   c. The real power of the ouija board comes from our subconscious minds; we don't know we're making it happen, but we are.
   d. Ouija puts us in touch with our friends who are dead.

Compare the different groups' results. Stress that sometimes we'll come to different conclusions because we're dealing with an area about which not much is known (the word 'occult' means 'hidden'); but we must remember that there are several possibilities – some of which are extremely dangerous. So we should be very careful about our attitude to any such phenomena, and always bear in mind verses such as 1 John 4:1–3; Isaiah 47:12–15; Matthew 24:24; 1 Timothy 4:1.

You may wish to talk a little about specific activities which you believe are dangerous (make sure you have good reasons to support your view). But avoid the temptation to elaborate with lots of 'scare' stories – you may be feeding an undesirable interest!

Activity (10 minutes)

If God is stronger than evil, why does it have such power in our world? The great theologian Oscar Cullmann compared it to the situation of Europe between D-Day and VE-Day: the outcome of the World War 2 struggle was certain, but the 'mopping-up operation' still had to take place. The decisive victory over evil happened with the cross. But VE-Day will arrive when Jesus returns.

Draw up a large chart in two columns, headed 'After D-Day' and 'After VE-Day'. List in each column things which are, or will be, true of life at that time. (For example: after D-Day murder, wars, volcanoes, etc, are still facts of life; after VE-Day there will be no killing, nature will be restored to harmony, etc.) You may want to give the group some biblical references (Isaiah 11:1–9, or Revelation 21:1–4) to help them with the VE-Day column. And you may want to ask the question: What's the difference between 'After D-Day' and 'Before D-Day'? In other words, what difference has the cross already made?

Game (10 minutes)

Give everybody a piece of paper which contains the following four possible reactions to the question of evil:
1. 'There's no such thing as the devil – it's all imagination.'
2. 'The only thing that's wrong with the world is human beings.'
3. 'If you get into the grip of Satan, there's no hope for you – the power of evil is irresistible.'
4. 'Communicating with the spirit world is a good way of gaining helpful advice.'

Hang on the wall cards containing the following verses (depending on the ability of your group, you may want to give them just the reference, or write the whole thing out): 1 Peter 5:8, Ephesians 6:12, Romans 8:38–39, Isaiah 8:19.

The group have to find the verse which gives an answer to each of these statements. To make it more confusing, add some cards which are quite irrelevant such as Isaiah 7:18, 1 Chronicles 9:39, Revelation 18:12. And to make it more interesting, lock a prize (eg a bar of chocolate) in a briefcase with a combination lock. Write one number of the combination on each of the four 'correct' cards (plus fake numbers on the 'incorrect' ones!), so that as people collect the correct verses, they are also collecting the number they need to open the case. The first group to open the case keeps the chocolate!

Bible story (10 minutes)

Use the 'Who's in charge around here?' sheet individually or in small groups.

Sketch: The prisoner (10 minutes)

Here's a sketch which is based on the temptation of Jesus by the devil (Matthew 4:1–10). One way to use it might be for two leaders to act it out, and then to ask the group: Which Bible story is this really about? Use the sketch to launch a discussion about:
- power: in what sense was the prisoner more powerful?
- temptation: how do these three temptations sum up the main ways in which the devil attacks our minds?
- evil: what was wrong in what the devil was offering?

(The prisoner sits bound to a chair in the doctor's interrogation room. The doctor, in a white coat, carrying a clipboard, paces up and down before him. The prisoner had been tortured and talks as if he is very tired.)

Who's in charge around here?

Read the story of what happened to Paul and Silas, two of God's special agents, in Acts 16:16–34. Then circle the letter of the answer which you think is right. Check your answers against what the Bible actually says – it's all in there!

1. The problem with the girl was that

    a she was a slave and had no money

    b she was possessed by an evil spirit

    c she was mad

    d she didn't have any problems, because she could see into the future

    e something else

2. Paul got rid of her problem by

    a commanding her to be quiet

    b commanding Jesus Christ to sort her out

    c commanding the evil spirit to come out of her

    d offering her a couple of Paracetamol

    e something else

3. As a result, Paul and Silas were

    a congratulated by everybody

    b treated with awe and fear by the girl's owners

    c able to get some peace for a change

    d flung into even deeper trouble

    e something else

4. But the most important outcome of the whole thing was

    a the girl's owners went bankrupt

    b Paul and Silas had some hymn singing practice

    c a whole family was converted and God's agents were freed

    d the architecture of the prison was altered a bit

    e something else

God's power will always protect his people, and always come out on top – even if at times it doesn't seem that way! And God's power is able to cope with all sorts of evils: supernatural problems such as the girl had, and natural difficulties like prison sentences!

THE DOCTOR: Power! Don't talk to me about power. How much power have you got?

PRISONER: More than you.

DOCTOR: More than me? Hah! *(Slaps the prisoner.)* How long have you been at the Institute?

PRISONER: I don't know.

DOCTOR: Forty days, that's how long. Forty days and forty weary nights.

PRISONER: But you haven't won. I haven't given in.

DOCTOR: Not yet! Not yet! But with our methods … our technology … our thought scanners and our mind-warping drugs …

PRISONER: You have no power. I am the powerful one.

DOCTOR: And where do you get this power from, may I ask?

PRISONER: From the Controller.

DOCTOR: The Controller! Oh yes! And you claim to be a favourite of his, don't you. But he hasn't turned up to help you in six weeks.

PRISONER: I know my instructions. I will resist.

DOCTOR: Oh no you won't. Look here. *(He punches a computer keyboard.)* The screen. What do you see?

PRISONER: Loaves … loaves of bread.

DOCTOR: Crusty, aren't they. Golden, warm. Freshly baked. Forty days since you had one. Would you like one now? *(The prisoner is silent. The doctor brings his face close.)* Now what do you see?

PRISONER: Pebbles …

DOCTOR: And you have the power, don't you! Prove it, then! Focus your mind … concentrate … turn the stones to bread!

PRISONER *(shaking his head)*: No. No. I can't.

DOCTOR: Aha! You can't! No power!

PRISONER: No. I know my instructions. Life is more than bread. The Controller says so …

DOCTOR: Pathetic evasion. Never mind *(He punches the buttons again.)* Now look. What do you see?

PRISONER: An aerial view … it's … I think it's the city … but so far below …

DOCTOR: A long way, isn't it? But you have the power! Jump! Let the Controller's power rescue you!

PRISONER: But I …

DOCTOR: Jump!

PRISONER: I won't.

DOCTOR: You can't, you mean.

PRISONER: I won't. I know my instructions. The Controller mustn't be put to the test.

DOCTOR: Oh! *(He throws his hands up in despair, then turns savagely to the prisoner.)* Very well, very well. I was hoping it wouldn't come to this. Obviously you need the ultimate treatment. *(He punches buttons furiously.)*

PRISONER: What are you going to do to me?

DOCTOR: Just look. On the wall scanner. *(He frees the prisoner, then spreads his arms to indicate the panorama which has just opened up, and remains standing motionless with his arms extended.)*

PRISONER *(softly)*: All the kingdoms of the world …

DOCTOR: Beautiful, aren't they?

PRISONER *(standing up slowly)*: All the wealth and power they contain …

DOCTOR: And it can be yours.

PRISONER *(turning to the Doctor)*: Mine?

DOCTOR: All yours. You can have it all. The moment you sign this paper and make a treaty with me. *(There is silence for a very long time. The two men stand staring at one another. Finally the prisoner looks away.)*

PRISONER: No.

DOCTOR: No? You can't say No. To all the power in the world?

PRISONER: I serve only the Controller. Not you.

DOCTOR *(becoming exasperated)*: The Controller, the Controller! Nothing but the Controller! *(He stabs his finger at the prisoner.)* You wait. You think you're so powerful. You're wrong. I'll be back. I'll think of something. You will lose. Oh yes! Because I have the power!

(Exit. The Prisoner looks thoughtfully after him for a moment.)

PRISONER *(softly)*: Power? Why talk to me about power? What power has he got? *(He stands up and extends his arms. Freeze.)*

Songs

I will build my church
Shine, Jesus, shine
He that is in us
Majesty (*Mission Praise* 151)
In heavenly armour (*Mission Praise* 79)
Thanks be to God (*Mission Praise* 577)
There is power in the name of Jesus

Action plan (15 minutes)

Read together Philippians 4:4–8 and make the point that the secret of combatting evil personally lies in controlling our minds. Depending on what we fill our minds with, we will have more or less power to stand against evil. An old Chinese proverb says: 'You can't stop birds flying over your house – but you can stop them nesting in your hair.' We can't escape evil things drawing themselves to our attention, but we can avoid focusing on them and letting them live in our imagination.

Divide a large poster up into four columns:

Brilliant   Good   Not so good   Deadly

Under each column, discuss and write down the kinds of things that have an impact on our minds for good or evil. 'Brilliant' includes positive spiritual input – Scripture, Christian books, time spent with God – and other things that improve our knowledge and awareness. Not all will need to be specifically Christian: finding out about victim support schemes could be a useful eye-opener! 'Good' is harmless entertainment, good reading, etc. 'Not so good' is mindless or dubious entertainment. 'Deadly' is actively harmful material: pornography, occult literature, sexist or racist or anarchic music, etc.

Decide together on a one-week action plan – three steps you will take to give your mind a tonic! It may include something negative (such as not watching a certain programme or video) and should certainly include something positive (such as daily re-reading of a certain passage, or reading a good book instead of something less helpful). It could be different for each person. At the end of the week, share experiences.

5. Failure

Introduction

Minor problems in our eyes are often major crises for the average 11–13 year old. Self-consciousness, spots, clumsiness ... all these things can be seen in terms of 'failure'. Your group members' self-images are easily dented, especially when, all around them, the world's attitude towards failure is all too obvious. Peer group pressure and especially the media demand 'perfection' and of course, they never quite make it. The activities in this chapter help the group members to recognise their own self-worth, especially in God's eyes, as well as learning how to deal with failure in their lives. There is a telling sketchscript, which should provoke some helpful discussion, as well as games to help them laugh at their mistakes and learn from them. A true story and a poem all emphasise God's love for them – after all, every hair on their heads is numbered!

Icebreaker (10 minutes)

You will need: enough photocopies of the 'People search' sheet and pencils or biros for one each.

Give everyone a sheet and something to write with and explain that the object of the game is to get as many different signatures as possible within a given time-limit of, say, three minutes and that the person with the most boxes signed is the winner. When the time is up, compare the sheets. Ask the group if there were any boxes which no one could fill. Can any of the group spot the theme linking all the boxes? Of course they all refer to times of failure – some sillier than others, and some which leave us feeling worse than others. On an overhead projector acetate or a large sheet of paper, quickly brainstorm how failure can make us feel (eg silly, useless, embarrassed, upset, angry etc). Ask if there is anyone in the group who did not sign a box, or has never failed at anything. (If so, do they consider that they are perfect? Why not?!) Stress that we all experience failure at some time in our lives. It can leave us feeling negative about ourselves, but in this session we will see what God thinks about us, and how he can help us view ourselves more positively.

Activity (10 minutes)

You will need: a fake microphone, a large flower (real or man-made!) and a few prepared anecdotes of embarrassing moments. (If you're stuck, useful sources include extracts from the following books: *The Book of Heroic Failures* by Stephen Pile [Penguin]; *Rolling in the Aisles* by Murray Watts [Marc Europe]; *Bats in the Belfry* by Murray Watts [Minstrel Publications].)

Using the microphone, launch straight into this activity with 'patter' along the following lines: 'Good afternoon, ladies and gentlemen. Welcome to the recording studio for the latest edition of our new radio series "Big Bloomers". Please could I ask for your cooperation as we prepare to go on air. Now let's start our programme with the following "Big Bloomers". (At this point, read out one or two of the prepared anecdotes, or get group members to read them.) Now it's over to our studio audience. Do we have any stories that anyone here would like to share with us?' Encourage the group members to share (maybe in twos or threes) times when they have wished the floor would open up and swallow them! You may find they will be more forthcoming if you share a mega-mistake you've made! If you have been working in small groups, have a time of feedback before announcing who has won the 'Big Bloomer' award. (You will need to handle this sensitively and keep it light-hearted or it may do more harm than good. Encourage the group to laugh *with* each other rather than *at* each other.) At the end of the session refer back to the results of the brainstorm on how failure makes us feel. Lead into the next activity, which looks at the opposite of failure – success.

Activity (15 minutes)

You will need: a ladder (if you can't get hold of a real one, a cardboard cut-out will do), Bibles, plain sticky labels for the rungs (address labels are about the right size) and thick felt pens.

Ask the group to suggest the names of people who have been a great success in the eyes of the world at some time. (Suggestions could include Princess Diana, Michelangelo, Winston Churchill, Michael Jackson, Charlie Chaplin, Shakespeare, Frank Bruno etc.) What are some of the things which make a person successful? (Skill, good looks, money, ability, charm etc.) As the group suggest different things, they could write them on the labels and stick them to the rungs of the ladder. What else are we 'told', often through adverts and magazines, that we need to have to be a success? (Designer labels, fast cars, trendy hairstyles etc.) Add these suggestions to the labels and stick on the ladder as before. Now ask the group to number the labels in the order of importance 'the world' gives them and rearrange them on the ladder accordingly with the most vital nearest the top. Finally, add a label with the word 'me' written on it (perhaps in a different coloured pen) to the very top rung.

Explain to the group that often, as far as the world is concerned, success is all about pleasing ourselves, getting what we want and putting 'me' first. (You may like to point out that it's not guaranteed either – lots of people strive for and achieve everything mentioned on the rungs, but are still regarded as failures in the world's eyes.) Emphasise that

People search

Find someone who can sign each of the lines below. Try to get as many different names as possible before the time runs out …

I have tossed a pancake – and missed!

I've never won a prize at a party

I once got on the wrong bus or train

I took part in a quiz – and lost

I tried a swimming badge and didn't get it first time

I once cooked a meal and burnt it!

I started a long run but I didn't finish it

I arranged to meet a friend and was late

I know someone who failed their driving test

I queued for a ticket but I couldn't get one

I auditioned for a play or concert and I was turned down

I took an exam or test but I didn't pass

there's nothing wrong with being successful, but it can become too important in our lives and we can end up being selfish and feeling failures and dissatisfied with ourselves. It's a bit like money really – it's what you do with it and your attitude towards it that really matters: if you make it your goal, you never have enough.

What does God say about success? Turn the ladder over and ask the group to find the following Bible verses in twos or threes (you may like to have the verses written on labels and attached to the rungs on the other side of the ladder in advance): Joshua 1:8; Proverbs 2:1–8; Isaiah 28:29; Luke 12:29–31; Colossians 3:1–2; Colossians 3:12–14; 1 Timothy 6:9–11; 2 Peter 1:3–8.

When each small group has found their verses, read them out in turn, stopping after each group to pick out key words from the verses which could be written on sticky labels and stuck on the rungs of the ladder. (Joshua 1:8, for example, could be summarised as: 'Obey God's Law, the Bible'.) After all the verses have been read out, ask the group to decide what should be put on the top rung of the ladder! (If you have time, you could turn the ladder back to the other side and see which labels could be transferred to God's way of living – not all worldly attitudes are wrong, by any means!) You could conclude with the well-known acrostic JOY (Jesus first, Others next, Yourself last) or read Romans 12:2 to the group.

Talk outline (7 minutes)

You will need: a round balloon, a water-based felt pen and a damp cloth. (If you feel that your group could take part in this experiment without it getting out of hand, with balloons being let off at the wrong moment etc, then all the group members could have a balloon and felt pen each. You will need to keep it very structured and explain the importance of conducting the experiment in a disciplined manner! You have been warned!)

Explain to the group that you (they) are going to perform a mini-experiment to discover how God can help us when we fail. Blow up the balloon and hold it *without* tying a knot. Ask the group to think of a time recently when they have done something which has left them feeling a failure – it may have been an action, a conversation or a thought. Ask them to tell the group about it (if they dare!) and write one or more examples on the balloon. On a given signal (maybe a 'count-down' with the group) release the balloon and watch it fall to the floor. Ask the group members to describe the state of the balloon! Explain how we can often feel deflated and useless when we make mistakes, but that one person who doesn't give up on us is God. Blow the same balloon up again, tying a knot this time. With a damp cloth, wipe the writing off the balloon, explaining that God cares for us even though we make mistakes and forgives us and helps us if we want him to. (If appropriate for your particular group, you could draw the analogy of God 'breathing' his Spirit into our lives.) Of course it doesn't mean we'll never fail again but we can be sure of God's love and forgiveness if we ask for it.

Sketchscript: One of those days! (5 minutes)

Scene: a one-sided telephone conversation.
Props: a telephone and some computer print-out paper (to give the impression of a very long list – it could contain the script!). A chair and a table with paper, pen and a mirror on it.
Character: the 'moan-machine' – a non-stop talker, sitting in front of a mirror looking depressed and inspecting a lump on his or her forehead.

The phone rings off stage (someone doing a good phone impersonation would do!) Enter moan-machine, who picks up the phone and starts on the monologue.

MOAN-MACHINE: 'Hello, this is the moan-machine speaking. I'm afraid I'm not in any fit state to answer your call at the moment, but if you'd like to leave your name and number I'll ring you back when I'm feeling more positive and less of a failure. Please speak after the tone *(pause)*. Oh on second thoughts, perhaps you'd just hold the line while I tell you what an awful day I've had. Is that OK?

Well, it's difficult to know where to start really *(unrolls paper as if reading a list)* – each bit's been as bad as every other bit. Talk about getting out of bed on the wrong side. Well, I really did today. Rolled over and leapt into a life-sized poster of Michael Jackson … and the solid wall behind it. No joke at that time of day. I've still got the lump to prove it. Then it was breakfast and I opened the Beddy Wreck, sorry Ready Brek at the wrong end, all over the floor! The dog quickly did his vacuum cleaner impersonation and mum her raving monster impersonation. In fact I arrived at school late of course, a wall-battered, hungry, deafened wreck and the day had only just begun! The wall wound was noticed by Brenda Briggs of all people, and did she give me some stick? It was really embarrassing. I felt so self-conscious, her good looks make me feel I look like a cabbage at the best of times. How would you have felt? Oh yes, the Maths test. Guess who got the most wrong? I'm sure that bump on my head has deadened my mathematical brain cells. Mind you, they were probably never very much alive anyway. I won't keep you, but I must just tell you about PE.

Of all the days to do the heats for Sports' Day. I was so useless Miss Johnson suggested I might try running backwards next time instead. Very funny! After dinner the wall wound was so obvious that Brenda Briggs kept asking in a very loud voice why I'd stuck a tomato on my head. Of course everyone laughed. I laughed along with them, but it really hurt inside. In fact the whole day really hurt. Do you ever have days like that? And now I've got to face tomorrow and the prospect of another day at school with this tomato on my forehead on show to everyone. I feel so stupid. I feel a real failure.

Oh, by the way, did you have a message for the moan machine? I'll just jot it down. 'Leave all your worries with him, because he cares for you.' Oh! *(Repeats the message much slower as if realising the meaning)* Leave all your worries with him because he cares for you. Oh thank you. That's very helpful. I just wish you had told me earlier in our conversation. What do you mean, you couldn't get a word in? Anyway, thanks. *(Quietly and thoughtfully)* … because he cares for you. For me. He cares for me. Leave all my worries with him because he cares for me' *(Puts phone down slowly and freezes).*

Reflections

1. Things that I like about myself …

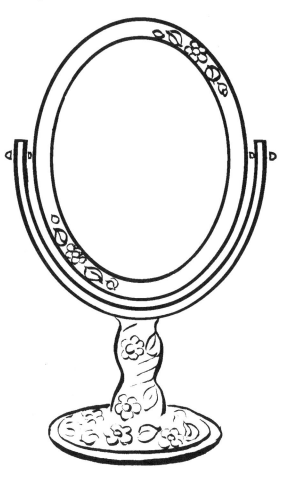

2. Things that I don't like about myself …

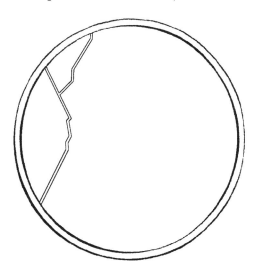

3. Matthew 10:30

Can you work out something God knows about you which shows just how much he values you?

4. Read Psalm 139:1–16 to find out about God's care for us – it's mega-amazing!

Choose just one phrase from these verses and write it in the mirror to remind yourself how special you are to God.

Follow up discussion (7 minutes)

1. What things had made the moan-machine feel so badly about his/her day and, more importantly, about him/herself? (Events at home and school and his/her appearance)
2. Can you suggest any other examples in these three areas which can have a similar effect on us? (Our appearance, spots, blushing, a haircut we don't like, problems at home, splits with friends at school etc)
3. What can we remember when our opinion of ourself is at rock bottom? (God cares for us)
4. What did the phone message tell us we have to do? (Leave our worries with him – ie tell God about things that are bothering us and making our lives a misery)
5. What other practical things could we do when we're having a bad day? (Talk to a friend, try and help someone else and take our mind off our own problems etc)

Funsheet (15 minutes)

You will need: enough photocopies of the 'Reflections' funsheet, pencils and Bibles for everyone to have one.

Hand out the fun sheets and ask the group to complete the first mirror. Tell them not to be too modest as no one else needs to see what they are writing (or drawing). Suggest that the really shy ones use their own code so that it doesn't make sense to anyone else! In the second mirror, with the crack, ask them to put some things they don't like about themselves. (You may find they are more forthcoming if you complete a sheet too …) In both cases, encourage the group members to try and think about more than just appearance – they could include personality, particular gifts, interests, attitudes to others and good or bad habits.

Now, using mirror number three, find the reflected Bible verse and discover a clue as to how much God knows you and cares about you … Before continuing, you may like to read this short poem (by Joan Brockelsby from *A Touch of Flame*):

Hair 543 …

Hair 54329635 fell out today.
God noticed.

Move on to the fourth mirror. If appropriate, ask a few group members each to read a section of the passage or read it yourself (it does need to be read well and slowly!). Ask the group which details of their lives are mentioned in these verses? (You could jot them down on an overhead projector acetate or a large sheet of paper: our thoughts [vs 1,2]; actions [v 3]; words [v 4]; whereabouts [vs 7–10]; bodies and feelings [vs 11–16].)

As suggested on the sheet, encourage the group to choose one phrase from the psalm which reminds them how much God values them and write it in the mirror. Finish by using the prayer/worship idea which follows.

Prayer/worship idea (5 minutes)

Suggest that the group spread out so that they are not too close to each other and, with eyes closed, quietly in their minds tell God what they like and dislike about themselves, thinking in particular about what they wrote down in their 'mirrors'. If appropriate, you could read 'Jesus take me as I am' (*Mission Praise* 127) as a poem, or maybe have a time of singing at this point, using some of the songs from the list below. Either you or a group member could pray this prayer:

Dear Heavenly Father, you know the things we like and don't like about ourselves. You know how we feel when things go wrong and we feel a failure. Thank you that you care about us so much that you even know how many hairs we have on our heads. Wow, that's amazing! Thank you that you have always known all about us. Thank you that you never stop loving us, even though we aren't very lovable sometimes, and we do things we shouldn't. Thank you that if we come to you and are really sorry, you forgive us and help us to start all over again. That's great. Thank you for the psalm which tells us about your love and care for us, especially … (at this point, the group members could quietly say their chosen phrase which they wrote in the mirror, either in their minds, or out loud in turn.) Please help us to love you and to love ourselves and each other in the way you want us to. Amen.

Songs

Father God, I wonder how I managed to exist
  (*Mission Praise* 348)
God is good (*Mission Praise* 370)
Jesus put this song into our hearts (*Mission Praise* 457)
Jesus take me as I am (*Mission Praise* 127)

Activity (15 minutes)

The 'Transport check' sheet should provide some fun – and maybe a few surprises!

Videos

McGee and Me – A Star in the Breaking Another mixture of animation and live action to help viewers apply biblical principles to everyday life. In this episode, Nicholas lets his appearance on TV go to his head and he has to learn the value of being humble. (30 minutes – CRP)

Hitch Hiker's Guide to Eternity. Guide 3. Part 5: Failure and Success Another burning issue for the editorial staff at the Guide's office to sort out! (20 minutes – CRP)

Take a look at these methods of transport. Which one of these vehicles do you think best describes you? Before you make your choice, think about your looks, personality, moods, likes and dislikes and strengths and weaknesses. Remember, you're not saying which one you **like** best, but which one is most like you! When you have decided, DON'T tell anyone just now which one you've chosen, but follow the instructions at the bottom of the page.

Circus clown's car –
full of fun and pranks

3-wheeler! – unpredictable,
but a bit different from the rest

Porsche –
cool, fast and image conscious

Pushbike – out of doors style,
content with a gentle pace

'Go anywhere' Jeep –
carefree and action packed

Make-believe 'Cinderella' coach –
dreamy, full of fantasy and very ornate

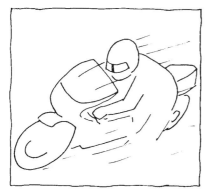

Motorbike –
daring and adventurous

Camper van – practical,
well equipped and ready for anything

Now move among the group and find out what other people thought you chose, at the same time guess which method of transport they decided was most like them. You may find the results surprising. We don't always see ourselves as others see us! If you dare, tell people why you chose your particular vehicle and see if they agree!

True story (3 minutes)

The following extract from *Many Voices, One Voice* by Eddie Askew is reproduced by kind permission of the Leprosy Mission International.

Simon Weston was twenty years old when he was terribly burnt during the Falklands Campaign. He was a soldier waiting to disembark from a ship when it was incinerated by an enemy missile. Many of Simon's mates died. He survived, but only just. I watched an intimate and very moving TV programme about his later progress through hospital. His face is very badly scarred, and, even after skilled plastic surgery, very disfigured. His hands and fingers are severely disabled.

The first thing that came through on the screen was the wonderful resilience of the human spirit. During his months in hospital and subsequent rehabilitation there were times of depression and times when he screamed with pain. Mostly, though, one saw Simon's courage, his matter-of-fact acceptance of what had happened to him, and his strong determination to fight back to life.

But the most moving experience was to listen to his mother talking to him. Gentle, but persistent, just chatting about home, food, birthdays, she brought him stability and simple encouragement. And it was brimful with love. She saw the scarred face, the burnt body, but it was so apparent that she was looking through that, to the real person underneath, her son. Whatever had changed, his identity hadn't. She knew the real Simon, and loved him. That's the strength of human love, made in the image of God's.

Sketchscript (2 minutes)

You will need: two photocopies of the script and two narrators (A and B) to read the lines alternately, with a pause in between each pair.

A and B together: Succeed with failure!

A: Failure doesn't mean you've accomplished nothing …
B: It does mean you've learned something.

A: Failure doesn't mean you've been a fool …
B: It does mean you had guts to venture.

A: Failure doesn't mean you've been disgraced …
B: It does mean you were willing to try.

A: Failure doesn't mean you should give up …
B: It does mean you must try harder.

A: Failure doesn't mean you'll never make it …
B: It does mean it will take a little longer.

A: Failure doesn't mean God has abandoned you …
B: It does mean that God has a better idea.

A: Failure doesn't mean you're a failure …
B: It does mean you haven't succeeded yet.

6. Families

Introduction

With family life under threat, we need to help the group members to discover God's plan for family life and how it applies to their own family, whatever that family may or may not consist of. This issue will need sensitive handling. With marriage breakdown on the increase, it's more than likely that some of your group members will come from broken homes. Be careful not to refer to Mum *and* Dad – it may be Mum *or* Dad, or even someone else who is looking after them. Often children feel that it's their fault that their parents got divorced, and we may need to reassure them that it's not. The activities aim to show the value of family life and help the children to value their own family, as well as facing up to tensions within a family – inevitable as they approach adolescence! There are games, discussion questions, role-play ideas and some suggestions for family outings. It's always helpful to get to know the group members' families, and these events could provide the ideal opportunity …

Icebreaker (10 minutes)

My family questionnaire

Give out the 'My family' sheet at the beginning of your session. Encourage people to get up, move around and talk to each other. The aim is to help them to relax and tune into the session's topic. Set a time limit (about 5 minutes, depending on the size of the group) in which they have to complete as much of the questionnaire as possible. The winner is the one who completes most, with correct answers, in the allotted time. Follow up by talking briefly about the group's answers.

Icebreaker (10 minutes)

Quirky questions

Ask group members to think about their answers to the following four questions, first by themselves, then sharing their answers in groups of three or four. Either photocopy the questions, so that each person can have a copy, or write them up on an overhead projector acetate, or large sheet of paper.
- What is the strangest thing about your family?
- What do you like most about your family?
- What is the most frightening thing that ever happened to your family?
- What do you most dislike about your family?

Share some of the most amazing answers in the larger group!

Activity (15 minutes)

Help group members to draw their family tree!

If your group is entirely made up of young people with a fairly strong Christian commitment, you might like to try the following activity based on the family tree idea. Ask them to find out and then draw/write down their Christian family tree. For example, Jane Brown was converted as a result of her parents' witness; her mum went to a Scripture Union beach mission as a child and became a Christian there; her dad became a Christian because of a Christian school friend … and so on. The results could be shared with the whole group and lead to some interesting discussion about the Christian family and its continuity throughout history. (This activity could be done at home.) If your group members do not have strong Christian backgrounds you could look at natural family trees or you could, alone, share your 'spiritual history'.

Activity (15–20 minutes)

You will need: a large sheet of paper per small group, plenty of magazines and newspapers, lots of scissors, glue, crayons and felt pens (enough for each group).

Divide the group into threes and fours and ask each group to make a collage depicting either a 'happy family' or a 'sad family'. Perhaps allocate a type to each group so that they don't all opt for the same one! Allow 10–15 minutes for making the collages, then put them on display. When everyone has looked at the collages, follow up with these two questions:
- What makes families happy?
- What makes families sad?

Game (15 minutes)

Photocopy the simple drawings on page 33 to make as many sets of 'Happy Families' cards as you need for your group. The basic face is given. Make four photocopies of each and add your own detail to make them into 'Mr', 'Mrs', 'Miss' and 'Master' and, of course, add the appropriate name.

In groups of four or five, play a *quick* game of 'Happy Families' in the usual way. Follow up with discussion about how the characteristics of the various 'families' help or spoil real family life.

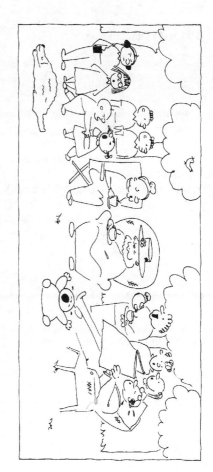

Who fits these descriptions? In the space provided, write the name of a person in your group who …

has a grandmother born before 1930

has one brother and one sister

lives with more people than anyone else

is the oldest child in their family

has a twin

has an older sister

is the youngest child in their family

has a member of his/her family who has been on TV

has a great-grandmother or great-grandfather still living

has a baby brother or sister

says their family never has arguments

has the most unusual surname

Happy family cards

The jealous family

The forgiving family

The mean family

The giving family

The cross family

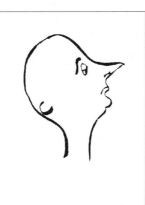

The proud family

The happy family

The loving family

Bible focus (10 minutes)

Ask the group:
- Why did God put us in families?
- What are families for?

Ask the group members to sit in a large circle and write down their own suggestions on a large piece of paper, placed in the centre of the circle.

Read Genesis 1:27–28; 2:18–24. From these verses you could make these points:
- God has given us families so that we are not lonely: ie for companionship (see 2:18).
- God has given us families to care for children in a way which will help them to grow up into adults who will care for his world (see 1:28).

Bible focus (20–25 minutes)

You will need: Bibles, pens and enough photocopies of the 'Lost son' sheet for everyone.

Read Luke 15:11–32 in parts (narrator, younger son, father, servant, elder son).

Give out the 'Lost son' sheet. Depending on the size and character of the group, you could either work in small groups of four or five with people sharing their answers in their groups followed by some whole group feedback, or you could lead the whole group through the worksheet, giving time for individuals to fill in answers and then have some whole group feedback and discussion of points raised.

Drama (25–30 minutes)

Photocopy the list below or write it up on an overhead projector acetate or a large sheet of paper. Ask the group members to pick out anything in the list which has recently caused an argument in their family.
- An untidy room
- Clothes
- TV programmes
- Videos
- Your friends
- Food
- School work
- Helping around the house
- Music
- Being unkind to brothers/sisters
- Money
- Other

Talk briefly about what they have chosen.

Divide the group into pairs and ask each pair to make up a sketch based on a disagreement about one of the situations in the list.

Depending on the size of the group, either ask all the pairs to show their sketches to the whole group, or select two or three pairs to show their sketches to the rest of the group.

Follow-up discussion questions:
- What were the real reasons behind the argument? (For example an argument about an untidy room may really reflect selfishness, tiredness etc.)

- How was or how could the situation have been put right?
- What does the Bible say? Read the following verses to the group: Exodus 20:12; John 13:34–35; Ephesians 6:1–4; Colossians 3:20–21.
- How could you deal with these situations in real life, if they happened at home?

Prayer ideas

Conclude the session with a short prayer time. You could use this simple outline for a time of silent prayer.
- Saying 'Sorry'. Is there anything you need to put right in your family/ask God's forgiveness for?
- Saying 'Please'. Is there anything you want to ask God for to do with your family?
- Saying 'Thank you'. What do you especially want to thank God for about your family?

Special events

Organise a family event of some kind, for example a:
- Pancake race.
- Fun run.
- Sports day.
- Summer barbecue/picnic.
- Concert.
- Quiz evening.
- Treasure hunt on foot or bike, or in parents' cars.

Videos

Cry from the Mountain Larry Sanders was about to break the news to his son that their home would be split up through divorce, when a serious accident and a series of frightening events changed everything. (75 minutes – CRP)

Runaway In this modern-day version of the story of the prodigal son, Colin runs away from home because he thinks his parents don't love him. (12 minutes – Scripture Union)

Lost son returns in sorry state
Father says 'I forgive you'!

Read Luke 15:11–32

Who disappointed his father? (Circle any of the answers which you think are right and write alongside the verse(s) which show your answer is right.)

Disappointment

The younger son   vs   ....

The servant   vs   ....

The pig farmer   vs   ....

The elder son   vs   ....

How did he/they disappoint his/their father? Circle any of the following which caused problems in the family:

Selfishness

Greediness

Being unloving

Jealousy

Rivalry

How were things put right? (Write your answer in the space below.)

....

....

Forgiveness

Forgiveness is two-way. One person says 'Sorry'. The other person says, 'That's all right – I forgive you'. Then both people's actions have to show that what they said is true. Answer the following questions in your own words. (Verses 18–21)

What did the younger son say to show he was sorry?

....

....

What did he do to show he was sorry?

....

....

What did the father say and do which showed that he forgave his son completely? (Verses 20–24)

....

....

7. Friends

Introduction

A board game, 'Fact files', 'How to be a good friend' fun-sheets, and discussion questions, as well as focusing on the type of friend Jesus was, all help to show what real friendship is about. It may be that your group members know each other well and are friends; or on the other hand, they may not all go to the same school, hardly know each other, and possibly be at loggerheads! Either way, these activities will help the group to get to know each other better and to become friends.

Icebreaker (10 minutes)

You will need: four or five large sheets of coloured paper or wallpaper, four or five glue sticks or tubes of glue, lots of pairs of scissors, other felt pens, as many other sheets of coloured paper as possible and catalogues (old mail order catalogues are best but the groups may have to share these).

Divide the group into four or five smaller groups and give each group the large sheets of paper, along with glue, scissors, paper and catalogues.

Ask them to write 'A friend is someone who …' at the top of their large sheet of paper and give them about 10 minutes to complete a poster. They can draw shapes and write on them ('… walks home from school with you' could be written on a foot shape, etc) or do ordinary drawings or cartoons, or just write phrases, or cut pictures from the catalogues ('… who invites you to watch a video' could be illustrated with a picture of a television etc.) In other words, they can do whatever they like, as long as their poster tells us about the things friends do together! When the time is up, display the posters and briefly discuss the positive aspects of friendship which they portray. Perhaps you could draw attention to the fact that friendships can be made up of normal everyday events, done with other people – it's *doing* things together that can help to build friendships …

Icebreaker (5 minutes)

Read Genesis 2:18 and point out that friendship was originally God's idea! Ask the group to get into twos (or threes) and give them a minute each to tell their partner what their best ever experience of friendship has been, or to say who they would give their 'World's most brilliant friend' award to, and why. After a minute, get them to swop over. If appropriate, get the groups to feed back (very quickly!). Maybe it would be worth pointing out that not everyone has one 'best' friend, some people have several very close friends (and not necessarily all the same age – friends can be much older or younger!).

Quiz (10 minutes)

You will need: photocopies of the 'How do you rate as a friend?' sheets – enough for each group member and enough pencils for everyone.

Give the group a time limit of, say, three minutes and ask them to tick one answer for each question. When the time is up, ask them to add up the number of a, b and c answers. If they have chosen all a's, they're either not being very honest or they are too good to be true! Mostly b's have got things about okay – they are thoughtful for other people but expect some consideration in return. Those who chose mostly c answers think too much about themselves – they'll need to change their attitude if they want to make and keep friends!
   Ask the group:
- Do you think we *choose* friends? (Not usually. On the whole, friendships 'develop' as people get to know each other, but the group members might still be at the stage where friends tend to be more temporary and people 'choose' to be friends in the school playground, for example. It will be interesting for you to find out what your group members think!)
- How do people make friends? (By spending time with each other, sharing interests and having things in common, although opposites can be drawn to each other! At school the group members might well go around in a group or gang of several friends. It might be worth pointing out that this can be exclusive, and maybe they could be encouraged to be aware of shy or lonely people, or newcomers.)

Bible focus (15 minutes)

You will need: a copy of the 'What kind of friend are you?' chart either on an overhead projector acetate or on a large sheet of paper, different coloured felt pens and enough Bibles, pencils and scrap paper for three small groups to use.

Divide the group into three. Give each small group a list of Bible references to look up, with questions against each. (Blank out the 'answers' if you copy the questions!) Group A will explore what the Bible has to say about making friends, Group B will deal with how we should treat friends and Group C will consider how to keep friends (although there will be 'overlap' in each group). Give a time limit of, say, five minutes and then report back and get each group to write their findings on the chart in the appropriate places.

Group A. How to make friends
Proverbs 18:24 What is an important part of friendship?
   (loyalty)

How do you rate as a friend?

1. Someone tells you they know something nasty about a friend of yours. Do you …

a Refuse to listen?

b Let them tell you, but keep it to yourself?

c Make sure you get the whole story and pass it on to as many people as possible?

2. What attracts you first in a person …

a The way they treat others?

b The way they treat you?

c Their looks?

3. Someone is talking about something on which you have strong feelings. Do you …

a Wait until they've finished and then put your point of view?

b Interrupt them to say what you think?

c Refuse to listen?

4. Someone tells you you look a mess in some new clothes you have bought. Do you …

a Take a long hard look at yourself and see if they're right?

b Tell them you'll look any way you like?

c Point out a few faults in what they are wearing?

5. You meet someone for the first time. Do you …

a Expect to make them your best friend?

b Find out more about them?

c Show them how clever you are?

6. Some friends tell you they once played a dirty trick on you which you never found out about. They now want to tell you about it. Do you …

a Forgive and forget?

b Tell them it's best to clear the air?

c Get angry before you've heard what they have to say?

The tongue is …

Solve the wordsearch and you will find words that warn of the dangers of allowing the tongue to get out of hand. Search vertically, horizontally and diagonally to find all seventeen. Then check them out by looking up all the Bible references.

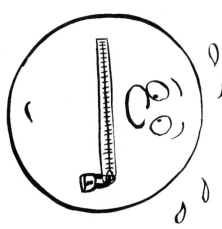

```
S O M U R D E R O U S D
S H A M E F U L A C G E
E U B P P E V I O N S S
L R O O V D C T S E I T
E T A I E R S C A D R T
R I L S N S I C O N N U
A N B O A P T O R S U C
C G O N E R I F N E O T
G N I S R U C I U I W I
C O R E G N A R Z L M V
G N I N I A L P M O C E
```

Destructive (Proverbs 18:21)

Gossip (Proverbs 18:8)

Lies (Proverbs 19:5)

Evil (Proverbs 17:20)

Fire (James 3:6)

Poison (James 3:8)

Cursing (James 3:10)

Critical (James 4:11)

Boastful (James 4:16)

Complaining (James 5:9)

Scorn (Proverbs 11:12)

Murderous (Proverbs 12:6)

Wounding (Proverbs 12:18)

Careless (Proverbs 13:3)

Shameful (Proverbs 13:5)

Hurting (Galatians 5:15)

Anger (Ephesians 4:26)

Proverbs 27:17 What benefits come from a good friendship? (learning from each other)

Proverbs 24:1 What kind of friendships should be avoided? (those with evil people)

Proverbs 22:24 What other friendships should be avoided? (friendships with violent people)

Group B. How to treat your friends

Proverbs 11:12 What needs to be avoided in a friendship? (being scornful)

Proverbs 12:26 What things do good friends and bad friends do? (guide, or lead astray)

Proverbs 11:13 How can friendships be spoilt? (gossip)

Proverbs 18:24 What makes friendships last? (loyalty)

Group C. How to keep your friends

Proverbs 16:28 What breaks up a friendship? (gossip, stirring up trouble)

Proverbs 17:9 What helps to keep friends together? (forgiving each other)

Proverbs 27:10 What else keeps a friendship together? (helping each other)

Proverbs 17:17 What do friends always do? (show their love and share problems)

What kind of friend are you?		
Making friends	Treating friends	Keeping friends
What kind of friend was Jesus?		
Making friends	Treating friends	Keeping friends

Bring the whole group back together and explain that you are going to find out what kind of friend Jesus was when he was here on earth. Encourage the group to contribute using their own knowledge of Jesus' life from the gospel stories. Depending on your group, you may like to refer to the following Bible passages: John 13:12–17; John 14:27–29; John 15:12–17, then see if the group can answer the three questions below and complete the chart as before. (Some guidelines are given in case you get stuck!)

How did Jesus make friends?

- He trusted his disciples with an important job.
- He was patient with his disciples.
- He was prepared to do things for them.

How did Jesus treat his friends?

- He expected obedience from them.
- He encouraged them.
- He was honest with them.

How did Jesus keep his friends?

- He forgave them when they made mistakes.
- He was thoughtful and noticed what they needed.
- He showed them his love – he was prepared to give his life for them.

Outside activities

Why not take your group on an outing? It can be great fun, and an excellent way to get to know each other better – a good way of demonstrating Christian fellowship! Here are some suggestions:

- A picnic – each group member could bring some food which could be 'pooled' so that everyone could share it.
- Swimming – always popular! If your group is large enough, you might qualify for a cheap group rate!
- A moveable feast – if you know the parents of your group members, they would probably be very happy to co-operate – you could start with the main course at one person's house, have the dessert somewhere else and end up for a drink at a third person's house!

Fun sheet (15 minutes)

Use the 'How to be a good friend' sheet or the 'The tongue is …' sheet individually or in small groups.

Game (15 minutes)

Point out to the group that friendships have their ups and downs and sometimes there are disagreements, and friends fall out with each other. Explain that this game will show us what the Bible says we should do when this happens.

You will need: two large jigsaws with about 24 pieces each (minimum needed is 18). You could either make these yourself using cardboard, or, alternatively, use the *backs* of two large children's floor jigsaws. They need to be prepared beforehand as follows:

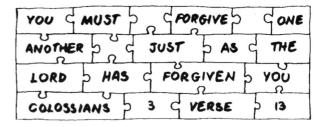

It doesn't matter where the 'blanks' are – they just make it more difficult!

Split the group in half and assemble the two teams at one end of the room, with the puzzles at the other end. Have a race, whereby each team member runs and collects a piece of jigsaw and when they return to their team, the next person runs to collect the next piece, and so on. Once all the pieces have been collected, the first team to assemble their jigsaw correctly is the winner and you can ask them to read the verse and answer the question, ' What does the Bible tell us to do

How to be a good friend

Can you put these items listed below in order of priority?
Number them from 1–12!

Being a good friend to someone means …

....	Listening to them when they have a problem
....	Visiting them when they are ill
....	Waiting for them when they are late
....	Stopping others making fun of them
....	Going to see a film with them which you've already seen
....	Lending them things they want to borrow
....	Talking to them on the telephone when your favourite TV programme is on
....	Being pleased for them when they do well at something you're hopeless at
....	Always accepting their apology when they have upset you
....	Never gossiping about them behind their back
....	Forgetting about things they have done in the past that upset you
....	Helping them and caring for them when they're worried or upset

If you can think of any other things that aren't on the list write them here!

....

....

Can you draw or write the name of one or more of your friends here?

Now, use this space to write down the things you like about them!

When you've finished this show it to your friends … if you dare!

when our friendships are spoilt by arguments or disagreements?' You could finish by reading the passage from which the verse is taken – Colossians 3:12–17.

Board game (10 minutes)

It may be that your group members know each other well and are already friends, but it's likely that some of them may be newcomers to the group and not all the same age and some may not live near each other or even go to the same school. This game will help you group members get to know each other a little bit better and maybe help them to become friends with each other – it's a useful group 'gelling' exercise!

You will need: four or five photocopies of the board game 'All about us!', the same number of dice and counters (or a suitable alternative) for each group member.

Divide the group into four or five smaller groups and give out the board games, dice and counters. Explain that they have say, eight minutes to complete the game, but they must answer the questions honestly when they land on a particular box! They will need to decide on a suitable forfeit (or maybe you can decide for them – something simple like singing a nursery rhyme usually works reasonably well!). Perhaps you could provide small prizes (something which could be shared with the rest of the group?!) for the winners.

Fact file (7 minutes)

These 'getting to know you' fact sheets are another way of encouraging the group members to get to know each other and to give the group a group identity. The group members could either complete them during the session, or take them home and bring them the following week. As far as a picture is concerned, they could draw one, cartoon-style, or provide a photo from home, or you could get a film and take the whole group individually, perhaps while they are working on another task, such as the board game. (Another idea would be to ask the group members to provide baby photos rather than up to date ones and then have a competition to see who can guess the correct babies!) If possible, do display the sheets once they are completed, and encourage group members to read each others fact files.

Prayer idea (10 minutes)

If the group would be able to cope with praying for each other, you could divide them into twos (or threes) and suggest they pray for the other person, either silently or out loud. They may find this embarrassing, so you could suggest that they shut their eyes! If more than two are in a group and they are happy to pray out loud, you could suggest that they pass a Bible around the group and the only person praying at any one time should be the person actually holding the Bible. This gets over the fear that two people might start to pray at the same time and gives people confidence! Alternatively, you could read a prayer for them to participate in quietly as follows:

Father God, thank you for all our friends. Thank you especially for … Thank you for the kind of people they are and the type of friend they are. Amen.

You could read the words of 'What a friend we have in Jesus' (*Mission Praise* 262) to close.

Activity (10 minutes)

Tell the group they are the panel of people whose job it is to answer letters sent to the problem page of a magazine. Ask them how they would set about answering a letter such as the one below.

> *Dear Problem Page,*
> *Please can you help me? My problem is that I haven't any friends, mainly because I am really shy and never know what to say to people – and when I do think of something it comes out wrong and sounds stupid. My family has just moved and I'm starting at a new school next month and I really want to make friends quickly. What can I do?*

NB This exercise needs to be taken quite seriously or you could end up making anyone who is lonely in your group actually feel worse rather than helping them! If you don't think your group could cope with it without turning it into a joke perhaps you as leader, could share with the group a time when you were lonely and mention anything that helped you (eg a Bible verse, a practical way of making friends etc).

Videos

McGee and me – Skate Expectations In this episode Nicholas learns the value of showing love and kindness. (30 minutes – CRP)

The Belonging Game Thirteen year old Wendy has moved to a new school and wants friends. But who and at what cost? (30 minutes – CRP)

The Tunnel Three kids and a grandfather team up to solve the mystery of a stolen racehorse, and in doing so discover that age is no barrier to friendship. (36 minutes – CRP)

The Green Bear This cartoon fantasy would be an excellent discussion starter about loneliness and friendship. Although it is designed for young children, you might get away with showing it to your group if you are totally honest with them and explain that although it is for little children, you thought it might be fun to watch together, as it has a lot to say about friendship!
(15 minutes – Scripture Union)

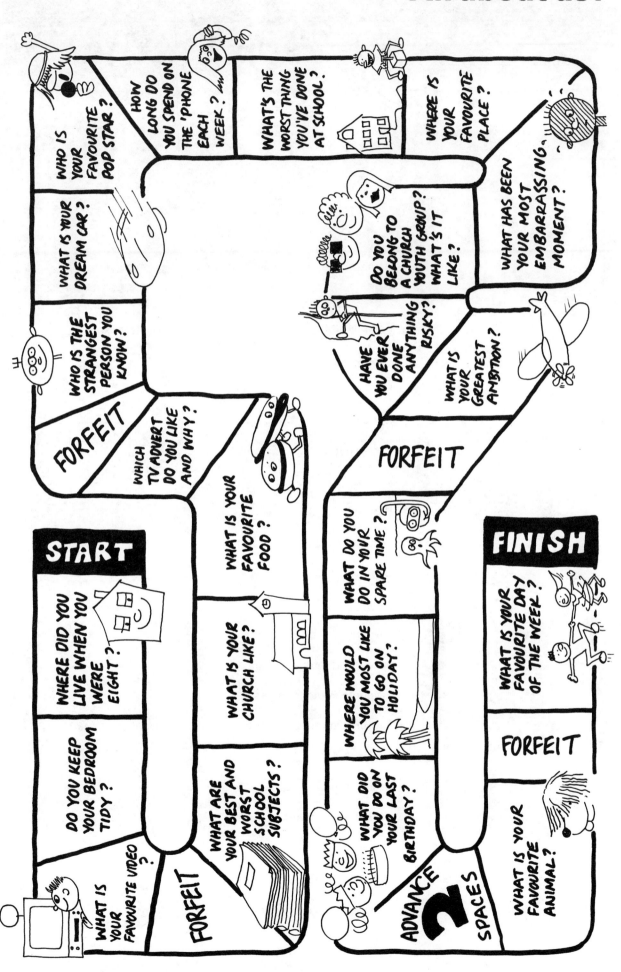

All about us!

Fact file

< Cartoon of yourself here, please!

Name ....

Date of birth ....

Birthplace ....

Height ....

Hair-colour ....

Eye-colour ....

Home address ....

....

I live with ....

Pets ....

Likes ....

Dislikes ....

Favourite group ....

Favourite record ....

Favourite TV programme ....

Favourite food ....

Heroine/Hero ....

Best Bible bit ....

School/Place of work ....

Bad habits ....

Hobbies ....

Favourite soap opera stars ....

8. Future

Introduction

Young people in the pre-teen years find it hard to think about the future. They probably haven't decided what they want to do when they leave school, and most find it difficult to imagine *anything* beyond the age of eighteen ... These activities will push back the boundaries a bit to help the youngsters think about their futures from a Christian point of view, and realise that God will be in control, whatever happens. Group members will eat a bar of chocolate with a knife and fork, glimpse the future with 'Weetaglimpse' – a new breakfast cereal, and hear some weather forecasts ... all guaranteed to get them thinking!

Icebreaker (10 minutes)

Our futures are as hard to predict as the outcome of this game!

You will need: one or two dice, a knife and fork, hat, scarf and gloves and a large bar of chocolate on a tray or paper plate.

To play the game, sit the group in a circle on the floor. The dice are thrown in turn around the circle (two dice may speed the game up a bit!). When a player throws a six, they run into the middle, put on the hat, scarf and gloves and start cutting up the chocolate with the knife and fork to eat *one piece at a time* with their fingers (for reasons of hygiene!). Once another person throws a six, they change places with the player in the middle, but they must have the hat, scarf and gloves on before they start to cut up the chocolate (using the knife and fork of course!) and eat it with their fingers. The game is over, needless to say, when all the chocolate has been eaten!

Ask the group:
- Was it easy to predict who would throw a six and go into the middle?
- Did it make any difference if someone was ready to act quickly if they threw a six?
- How can our lives be a bit like the game we've just played?

Questionnaire (10 minutes)

Explain to the group that you want them to be honest about their feelings about the future. The 'Feelings about the future ...' sheet lists a variety of things – some serious and others not so serious – which they may have to face soon, or in the distant future. Show them how to mark along the line given, to indicate how excited or worried they feel about the prospect of a particular thing happening to them. Explain that they won't have to show their answers to anyone else if they don't want to, so they can be really honest! Give them five minutes, to allow time for feedback.

As a group, or in twos and threes if more appropriate, share something you are really looking forward to, and also something you are afraid of, or really dreading.

Ask the group:
- Does anyone want to share something they are excited about and looking forward to?
- What about things in the future which we aren't looking forward to?
- How often do you think about what might happen to you as you grow up?

Finish this discussion by looking together at Jeremiah 29:11: 'I alone know the plans I have for you ...' (If you have a lively or restless group, part of this verse could be done as 'Hangman' on a large sheet of paper, but keep an eye on the time as it can take ages!) Suggest that group members learn it for the next session if they wish (perhaps offer them a small reward as an incentive!) as it can really help and encourage us to know that God cares about what happens to us. Maybe you could tell the group about a time when *you* have been in a difficult situation or needing guidance for the future, and God has helped you in a very specific way. Personal experiences shared in this way can be very powerful, and speak volumes to young people.

Activity (10 minutes)

If your group is ready for this type of activity, it follows on well from the questionnaire.

You will need: a long length of string, a piece of card for each group member to write their name on (so you may need pens) and two cards labelled 'ALWAYS' and 'NEVER' to go at either end of the string when it's laid out.

Sit everyone in a circle on the floor and lay the string and cards across the middle.

Each group member has to decide how much they would pray about a situation mentioned in the questionnaire, and then place their name card (or initials only if that is less threatening!) at some point on the line to show their answer. Give the group the following example to start off: 'Would you pray about a proposed new haircut?' If not at all, then the card would go next to the 'NEVER' label, if sometimes, then the card would need to be placed nearer the middle of the string line, and so on. The cards are picked up after each situation mentioned, and re-positioned for the next one. After a few turns, have an informal discussion about the responses and the sorts of things we do or don't consider praying about. You could refer to Philippians 4:6 and suggest that the group members think about one particular situation (big or small) they may have to face, and pray about it during the coming week.

Bible focus (5 minutes)

Have the following Bible verses written on slips of paper for willing volunteers to pick. Get them to find their Bible verse and then read it out in turn. Have a pause between verses and let the Bible speak for itself!

Jeremiah 29:11; 1 Peter 5:7; Matthew 28:20; Psalm 34:4; Isaiah 41:10; Hebrews 13:5–6; Psalm 143:8–10; Philippians 4:6–7; Jeremiah 33:3.

Sketchscripts (7 minutes)

Before introducing the first sketch ask the group what future events in the world can be predicted fairly accurately. Weather forecasts should be suggested! (If horoscopes are mentioned, and it's likely they will be, it's probably best to discuss that issue separately later and not get sidetracked at this point. The whole subject is dealt with in the section on 'Evil' on page 21.) How can we find out what the weather will be like tomorrow for example? As the weather forecast sketches are performed, encourage the group to listen and watch carefully as they will need to remember details for the next activity! After both sketches have been performed follow up with the quiz.

Weather forecast 1

Cast: weather reader; person A to give props; person B to wear props, standing on plastic sheeting (and prepared to get wet!).

Props: sunhat and sunglasses; balloon and pin; talcum powder; ice cubes; handkerchief; watering can and cup of water; snorkel, armbands and flippers; large sheet of plastic for B to stand on.

WEATHER READER: Good afternoon. Here is the weather forecast for today and tomorrow. Today we are all enjoying sunny weather in most parts *(A puts hat and sunglasses on to B)* which will continue throughout the day as high pressure increases. *(A blows up balloon in rhythmic gasps.)* Temperatures will soar this afternoon with a real bang! *(A pops balloon.)* We can expect the temperature to drop rapidly tonight, however, *(A removes hat and glasses from B)* with mist in most areas turning into thick fog in patches. *(A blows talcum powder across B's face, taking care to avoid his or her eyes!)* Visibility will be very poor and drivers are advised to go slowly and follow road signs very carefully. Into the night, temperatures will drop below freezing, so beware of ice in unexpected places *(A drops ice cubes down B's back!)* which may cause skidding for drivers. Take extreme care. Sadly, the outlook for tomorrow looks bleak, with low pressure bringing a great depression over everyone. *(A gives hanky to B who sobs bitterly.)* With it a light drizzle will start, *(A pours water from watering can over B's head)* which will soon turn to heavy rain *(A pours cup of water over B's head)* and there's warning of severe flooding *(A gives B snorkel, armbands and flippers to put on)* but there is no need for alarm. Otherwise the forecast looks quite settled, apart from the heatwave, fog, ice, rain and storms, so safe travels! Goodbye for now.

Weather forecast 2

Cast: weather reader; voice (to read italicised lines in brackets, if possible out of sight of the audience).

WEATHER READER: Good afternoon. Here is the weather forecast for today and tomorrow. *(Here is the long-range forecast for the rest of your lives!)* Today we are all enjoying sunny weather in most parts *(friends, fun, good health, opportunities, success, holidays)* which will continue throughout the day as the high pressure increases. Temperatures will soar this afternoon with a real bang! *(Jesus said, 'I have come in order that you might have life – life in all its fullness.')* We can expect the temperature to drop rapidly tonight however, with mist in most areas turning into thick fog in patches *(disappointment, let downs, vague promises, unclear direction, change of circumstances, spoilt plans, facing the future)*. Visibility will be very poor and drivers are advised to go slowly and follow road signs very carefully. *(Psalm 119 verse 105 says that the Bible is ' … a lamp to guide me and a light for my path.')* Into the night, temperatures will drop below freezing, so beware of ice in unexpected places *(temptations to lie, cheat, steal, blaspheme, fight and hurt)* which may cause skidding for drivers. Take extreme care. *('My help will come from the Lord. The Lord will guard you; he is by your side to protect you.' Psalm 121 verses 2 and 5.)* Sadly the outlook for tomorrow looks bleak, with low pressure bringing a great depression over everyone *(problems at home, break-ups with friends, bullying)*. With it a light drizzle will start, which will soon turn to heavy rain, and there's warning of severe flooding *(redundancy, failed exams, family splits, divorce, unemployment, death, damaged environment)* but no need for alarm *('Leave all your worries with him because he cares for you' – 1 Peter chapter 5 verse 7)*. Otherwise the forecast looks quite settled apart from the heatwave, fog, ice, rain and storms, so safe travels! *('I the Lord your God am with you wherever you go' – Joshua chapter 1 verse 9.)* Goodbye for now.

Quiz (5 minutes)

You will need: 20 childrens' building bricks (or plastic cups) and 20 paper plates.

Divide the group into two teams and choose a builder for each team. If their team answers a question correctly, they build a tower, using either one brick, or a plastic cup with a paper plate on top. The aim is to have the tallest tower at the end of the quiz! If one team can't answer the question it can be passed across to the others, but keep the whole thing moving along quickly! (If appropriate at the end of the quiz, you could draw a parallel between the towers and our lives. Eg just when everything seemed to be going smoothly it all came crashing down …!)

1. What was used in the sketch to represent sunny weather? (Hat and sunglasses)
2. What were we told the temperatures would do? (Soar with a bang!)
3. What things in our lives might represent sunny weather? (Fun, good health etc)
4. What did Jesus say he had come to give us? (Life in all its fullness)
5. What did the weather reader say would come in patches? (Thick fog)

6. What sorts of things in our lives might be like thick fog? (Disappointments etc)
7. What is like a lamp to guide us when the way ahead is difficult? (The Bible)
8. What will bring a great depression tomorrow? (Low pressure)
9. What sorts of things might make us depressed? (Problems at home etc)
10. Who can help us when life gets tough? (The Lord)
11. Where are we told to leave our worries? (With the Lord)
12. Who will be with us through all the various types of 'weather'? (God)
13. What were the weather readers opening words? (Good afternoon)
14. What did the weather reader wish us at the end of the forecast? (Safe travels)
15. How many items were put on to prepare for flooding? (Three)
16. What sorts of things represent severe floods in our lives? (Failed exams, death etc)

Activity (10 minutes)

You will need: a cereal box covered with paper and re-named 'Weetaglimpse'; photocopies of the 'Weetaglimpse' life charts (enough for one each), pens.

Ask the group to imagine that they have eaten a new break-fast cereal called 'Weetaglimpse' which has given them the ability to 'glimpse' very briefly into the future. When they have tasted this amazing new cereal they will be able to see what lies ahead for them way into the 21st century. (At this point you could brandish the cereal box for effect. Perhaps it could contain some sweets for the group members?!) Ask them to think for a moment about what they would like to see … a sports achievement? marriage? children? a hit single in the charts? Using the Weetaglimpse life charts ask the group members to write or draw on their charts any partic-ular events which they think might happen to them in the future, in the order they could happen. Use a time limit to force everyone into a speedy decision and help keep the atmosphere light-hearted! This isn't intended to be too ana-lytical – more of a thought provoking exercise! Now, using the symbols on the charts, ask the group to draw appropriate symbols next to each event they have drawn or written, to indicate how they are feeling about it. If the group could handle it you could suggest they compare notes in twos or threes. In conclusion you could refer to the Bible references given in the 'Bible focus' or refer back to the Weather fore-cast 2 sketch. If appropriate, prayers and suitable songs could be used at this point, or you could move on to the Prayer idea.

Prayer idea (7 minutes)

In this 'Prayer Consequences', the group will have an opportunity to offer their futures to God, and pray for each others hopes and fears if appropriate.

You will need: enough bookmark-sized pieces of paper and pens for each group member.

Give everyone their pen and paper. At the top of the paper ask them to write one thing which happened to them in the past – last week, last year, when they were small, good or bad. (In other words, anything, preferably the first thing that comes to mind!) Get them to fold the paper over at the top, so that what they have written is hidden, and pass it on to the person on their right (or left!). Next, ask the group to write something down which they have done today, on their new bit of paper. Again, the pieces of paper should be folded over from the top and passed on to someone else. Thirdly, ask everyone to write down something they have got planned for the future – perhaps tomorrow, next week, or even further ahead. Fold and pass on as before. Finally, ask every-one to write the words; Jesus said, 'I will be with you always' (Matthew 28:20) at the bottom of the paper. Then everyone can open up the pieces of paper they are holding and read the three episodes listed. You may want to encourage one or two people to read theirs aloud to the rest of the group. Point out that we have heard about a few snippets from people's lives, some of which might not have made any sense to us! God, however, sees everyone's lives fully – the past, present and the future too – all the bits we've not even lived yet! Although our futures stretch out before us as the great unknown, we *do* have the promise that Jesus will be with us (written at the bottom of their paper). You may like to finish with a prayer along these lines:

Father God, You know us all individually. You know our thoughts, worries and excitement about the future, especially (perhaps have a time of silence at this point, and then read out some or all of the 'Future' sections of the consequences just produced) Please help us to remember that you promise that whatever we face in the future, you will always be with us. Amen.

Songs

Be bold, be strong (*Mission Praise* 312)
Father God, I wonder (*Mission Praise* 348)
I do not know what lies ahead (*Mission Praise* 409)
Father I place into your hands (*Mission Praise* 45)
    Some of these songs are quite long. It may be better to select one or two verses and simply read them out as poems, rather than attempting to sing them!

Videos

Joseph This brilliant, award-winning video deals with the story of Joseph's life in four episodes. Lively and funny, it emphasises God's plan for Joseph's life, which worked out against all odds. A helpful discussion starter, it focuses on God's timing and his patience.
(18 minutes approximately x 4 – Scripture Union)
A Beginner's Guide to Revolution Sidney Penge desper-ately wants to pass his exams and so he resorts to prayer. This entertaining cartoon explores questions about and the possibilities of prayer, and how God cares about us and knows what is best for our lives.
(15 minutes – Scripture Union)

Weetaglimpse life chart

Add onto this chart any event you think might happen to you in the future.

Try and put them in the order they might happen.

Dream some dreams and be honest about any fears …

Symbols

(: :) = very positive
yippee!

(: () = very negative
ugh!

(: <) = very vague
err?

Year	Your age
2000	
2005	
2010	
2015	
2020	
2025	
2030	
2035	
2040	
2045	
2050	

Feelings about the future …

Mark along the line with a cross according to whether you feel excited, worry a lot or don't really care when you think about the following things:

	Worry a lot	Doesn't really bother me	Very excited
Growing up			
Getting a job			
Taking GCSEs			
Getting my hair cut			
Moving house			
Changing school			
Nuclear war			
Losing someone special			
Spending pocket money			
Having a party			
What to wear			
Leaving home			
Parents splitting up			

9. Global issues

Introduction

Question: What has cutting a cake into unequal portions got to do with global issues?

Answer: It demonstrates the unfair use of the world's resources by the rich.

Question: What has a life-sized board game drawn on the floor got to do with the Third World?

Answer: The players move around the board themselves, discovering something of what it is like to live in a Third World country.

These are two of the suggested ways in which you could help your group be more aware of the world we live in, and the need to take more care of it and the people who live in it. At the end of this session, we suggest that you draw up a 'Plan of Action' in response to what the group has learnt, particularly about the way God wants us to live.

Icebreaker (8 minutes)

You will need: a cake (or two!), a knife and a rubbish bin!

Produce the cake and cut it into very different sized pieces, making sure that there are not quite enough pieces for everyone. Hand pieces out to some of the group, having first taken a large piece for yourself! To add insult to injury, after a couple of mouthfuls, you could say, 'I can't eat all of this there's too much!' and put the rest in the rubbish bin. After everyone else has finished their piece, talk about what happened. Did people with big pieces share theirs with those who had small ones or none at all? Did those who missed out accept it, or complain loudly?

After the point has been made that it's often like this with the earth's resources, you could produce another cake, to give everyone their 'fair' share. Be sure to bring out the fact that this doesn't happen in real life there is only one 'cake' (earth) to go round. You could finish with the following quotes:

> The rich must live more simply so that the poor may simply live (Dr Charles Birch).

> ...The earth cannot afford, say, 15% of its inhabitants – the rich who are using all the marvellous achievements of science and technology – to indulge in a crude, materialistic way of life which ravages the earth (EF Schumacher).

Activity (10 minutes)

Use the 'How green are you?' sheet to get things started!

Bible focus (12 minutes)

You will need: an overhead projector acetate or a large sheet of paper with the Bible references written on, pens, Bibles for everyone (and pens and paper for each group would be useful).

Divide the group into six or eight* groups of two or three. Give each group one reference to look at and allow them, say, five minutes to summarise the passage, ready to report back to the others. When it's time for the feedback, get the group members to fill in the results on the OHP or sheet as they explain to everyone what their verses were about. Conclude by highlighting what the Bible says about God's world and the way we should live in it.

1. Genesis 1:1–2:4 (God creates the universe and is very pleased with it.)
2. Genesis 3:1–19 (People's disobedience, when it all started to go wrong.)
3. Genesis 8:20–22 (God promises to keep his world going.)
4. Psalm 8 (God puts people in charge of the world.)
5. 1 Timothy 4:4,5; 6:7,8 (Everything God created is good and we should be thankful – but not greedy or discontented.)
6. Romans 8:18–25* (God promises future renewal of creation.)
7. Colossians 1:15–23* (Our role as 'friends of God'.)
8. 1 John 3:16–18 (The responsibility to share.)

* These are quite difficult passages, so be careful which groups you allocate them to, if at all!

Activity (20 minutes)

You will need: large sheets of paper, old calendars, colour supplement magazines, picture postcards, newspapers and scissors, glue and felt pens. Also, leaflets, posters and publicity from organisations such as Tear Fund, Oxfam, Christian Aid and Friends of the Earth would be useful – see address list.

Explain to the group that they have say, fifteen minutes to produce a poster or collage, either individually or in small groups. Their poster should have two 'messages' – 'God created', 'Man destroyed'.

You will probably find that most of the group members will have their own ideas and be happy to get on without any prompting from you.

How green are you?

Ask other group members to sign on the dotted line if they …

Can say who the earth belongs to

Save aluminium cans for recycling

Can explain the meaning of the term 'Third World'

Can mend a bicycle puncture

Use recycled paper loo rolls

Take empty bottles to the bottle bank

Can name ten different birds

Can think of a good use for the back of this sheet of paper

Would be able to replace a zip, sew on a button or darn a sock

Would give some of their own money to help a Third World charity

Never drop litter

Would pick up litter dropped by someone else

Know why the rain forests are important

Bought recycled paper Christmas cards last year

Help with the gardening

Feed the birds in winter

Could replace a washer on a dripping tap

Have a good idea for how our group could support a Third World charity. (What is it?)

Could explain why it's important to insulate your home

Have a good idea for how our group can 'go green'. (What is it?)

Whose world is it anyway? Genesis 1:1

Game (15 minutes)

You will need: coloured chalks (or photocopies of the board game – enough for each small group to have one each – and enough counters for one per player), dice, one set of photocopies of the 'Bonus' and 'Hazard' cards (or one set for each small group).

Create your own board game to show the group what it must be like to live in a Third World country. Why not draw the huge 'track' (copied from the game drawn here) on the floor, using coloured chalks? The counters could become group members – great fun, a good learning exercise, more memorable and a bit different!

If your floor is unsuitable, and the weather is fine, how about going outside? A tarmac surface would be ideal (and available if you happen to meet in school or church premises). Even a domestic driveway might do! If it's out of the question, photocopy the game and play in small groups using counters. The rules are very straightforward: Players move the number of spaces indicated by the die and the first one to reach the end is the winner. Anyone landing on a Hazard or Bonus square takes a card and replaces it on the bottom of the pile after obeying the instructions. Over to you!

Bonus cards

A midwife was available to help with your birth.
Forward 2 places.

There's an immunisation programme in your area.
Forward 2 places.

You become part of a child sponsorship scheme and your schooling is guaranteed to age 12.
Have an extra turn.

You hear the Good News about Jesus' love for you and you respond to God's offer of forgiveness and a new life with him.
Forward 4 places.

You hear the Good News about Jesus' love for you and you respond to God's offer of forgiveness and a new life with him.
Forward 4 places.

There's a clean water supply in your village at last, thanks to a Tear-Fund project.
Forward 3 places.

Hazard cards

You were born in the slums of a Latin American city.
Miss 2 goes.

Your diet is very poor.
Back 3 places.

You have no education.
Miss 1 go.

You contract polio because you weren't immunised. There's no treatment available. You die.
Drop out of the game.

Floods devastate your crops.
Back 4 places.

Floods devastate your crops.
Back 4 places.

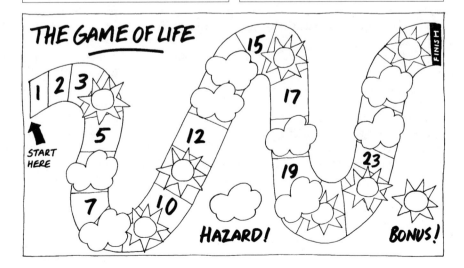

Outside activity

Organise a 'Rich man, Poor man' supper. (Maybe this could be held in a group member's home.) All the guests pay a flat rate for tickets in advance. This will give you an idea of numbers, as well as giving you a budget to work on so that you can aim to make a profit, which could be sent to Tear Fund, or some other relief organisation.

When the guests arrive, they are issued with vouchers which entitle a few to have a three course meal with all the trimmings and waiter and/or waitress service. Those partaking of this 'banquet' are seated at a table in the centre of the room, whilst everyone else, who aren't entitled to share the feast, sit around the edge of the room on the floor and are given a bowl of rice and a cup of water for their supper. Needless, to say it is a very effective visual aid!

After the meal, discuss briefly how it felt to be either eating the banquet or sitting on the floor with a bowl of rice. Did those in centre of the room feel guilty? Did they share their food with those less fortunate than themselves, or did they just consider themselves 'lucky'? Did those on the floor ask, or even beg, for food? Were they envious, or angry?

It would be appropriate to finish this session with a time of prayer. If the group members would be too shy to pray out loud, you could lead a time of quiet in which they could pray silently about what has just happened and their thoughts about it, but more importantly, about what is really happening in the Third World. End the prayer time by reading this passage:

> My brothers, what good is it for someone to say that he has faith if his actions do not prove it? … Suppose there are brothers or sisters who need clothes and don't have enough to eat. What good is there in your saying to them, 'God bless you! Keep warm and eat well!' – if you don't give them the necessities of life? (James 2:14–16).

Worship ideas

If you have or could borrow a collection of appropriate slides, the group could arrange a short slide sequence to accompany the reading of Psalm 104. In other words, the group could put together their own audio-visual presentation!

The psalm could be divided up as follows, with slides as suggested:
- Psalm 104:1–4 pictures of skies, dawn breaking, clouds etc.
- 5–9 seas and rivers
- 10–15 animals and birds, rain, grass, farmers harvesting crops
- 16–18 trees and forests, mountains
- 19–23 moon and sun, sunsets, wild animals
- 24–30 people
- 31–35 any pictures which portray God's majesty and glory

Psalm 8 is also a good psalm to read as a meditation, especially if you have any musicians in the group who could play softly in the background while it is being read. This could be followed with Psalm 9:7–12.

Songs

A new commandment I give unto you (*Mission Praise* 283)
Ascribe greatness to our God the rock (*Mission Praise* 14)
From heaven You came, helpless babe (*Mission Praise* 361)
He's got the whole world in his hands (*Mission Praise* 390)
Jesus is Lord (*Mission Praise* 119)
Let there be love shared among us (*Mission Praise* 137)
Make me a channel of your peace (*Mission Praise* 153)
Sing to God new songs of worship (*Mission Praise* 560)

Activity (30 minutes)

Organise a debate, with the motion being 'This house proposes that people in the West should accept a lower standard of living to benefit those in the Third World'. You will need two teams with a proposer and a seconder in each team. They will need to prepare their speeches 'for' or 'against' and you will need to elect a chairman to organise the proceedings. The proposer for the motion begins, followed by the opposer. The seconders for each side follow, then the debate can be opened to the 'house' for anyone who wishes to speak. The opposer then makes a closing speech, followed by the proposer. The chairman then puts the motion to the vote. (It sounds complicated, but it's really quite straightforward, and could be done without the 'seconders'.)

Activity

Why not suggest to the group that they draw up a 'Plan of Action' in response to the things they have learnt about the state of our world, and the plight of people in the Third World?

See what suggestions they come up with, but if necessary suggest they refer to the 'How green are you?' sheets they used for ideas of things they could do, as well as possibly writing to one or two organisations for ideas (see address list). If they do that, they may need of course to wait for replies before they make any plans. Encourage them to think in terms of practical things, some of which could be given to particular group members to do (eg a child which the group might sponsor would need to be written to on a regular basis). Of course, it would be good if they could commit themselves to some fund raising. It may be better if this was on a long-term basis, rather than anything too ambitious to start with!

Perhaps get the group members to make a poster or chart outlining their plans, so that they can work out a strategy and allocate specific tasks to particular people, or small groups. A useful book to refer to would be *The Blue Peter Green Book* published by BBC/Sainsbury's.

Fund-raising ideas could include: sponsored events, Smartie tubes full of coins, carol singing, table-top sales, shoe-cleaning, car-cleaning etc … Other action could include lobbying the local Member of Parliament for more Third World aid, or on local environmental issues.

Obviously it would be good to get the group praying about the things they have learnt from this session, in particular the needs of the Third World. Prayer 'triplets' are a good way to encourage the group members to pray together on a regular basis.

Useful addresses

Tear Fund, 100 Church Road, Teddington, Middlesex TW11 8QE. (It's probably worth explaining that the initials stand for The Evangelical Alliance Relief Fund. They produce excellent resources, including videos, and there is a good magazine for 11–13s called *On Target*. At only 10p per copy it's worth getting copies for your group members to link in with this session.)

Traidcraft plc, Kingsway, Gateshead, Tyne and Wear, NE11 0NE.

Christian Aid, PO Box 100, London SE1 7RT.

Oxfam, 274 Banbury Road, Oxford OX2 7DZ.

Aluminium Can Recycling Association (ACRA), I-MEX House, 52 Blucher Street, Birmingham B1.

Campaign for Lead-Free Air (CLEAR), 3 Endsleigh Street, London WC1H 0DD.

Department of the Environment (DoE), 43 Marsham Street, London SW1P 3PY.

Friends of the Earth, 26–28 Underwood Street, London N1 7JQ.

National Centre for Alternative Technology, Llwyngwern quarry, Machynlleth, Powys, Wales SY20 9AZ. (This centre experiments with 'alternative' energy, including wind power and solar energy.)

Royal Society for the Prevention of Cruelty to Animals, Causeway, Horsham, West Sussex RH12 1HG.

Woodland Trust, Autumn Park, Grantham, Lincs NG31 6LL. (Runs an excellent 'Plant a tree for £1' campaign.)

Worldwide Fund for Nature UK (WWF), Panda House, Weyside Park, Godalming, Surrey GU7 1XR. (Campaigns to save endangered animals.)

The Warmer Campaign, 83 Mount Ephraim, Tunbridge Wells, Kent TN4 8BS. (For fact sheets on paper, plastic, glass and other waste recycling.)

Centre for Environmental Information, 24 Roseberry Road, Cheam, Surrey.

Shell Better Britain Campaign, Freepost, Birmingham. (Information on community environmental projects.)

Videos

Mother Teresa and Her World An award-winning documentary about Mother Teresa and her work in Calcutta. (55 minutes – CRP)

Angel with a Bushy Beard Introduced by David Frost, this film is about the work of Major Dudley Gardiner who is involved in feeding the poor of Calcutta. (25 minutes – CRP)

Children on the Edge This award-winning video focuses on the problems children face in the Third World and shows how Tear Fund's development programme gives them opportunities to develop their full potential. (22 minutes – Tear Fund/CRP)

Getting to Work With special emphasis on the groups that supply beautiful handmade items for sale through Tearcraft, this video shows how people without jobs are being given employment, independence and dignity. (20 minutes – Tear Fund/CRP)

Water of Life This video can be used as an aid to meditation on God's provision of water for our needs. It is followed by a documentary-style programme about problems created by polluted water in Africa. (15 minutes – Tear Fund/CRP)

10. Happiness

Introduction

Happiness, like love, is often misunderstood. It's likely that your group will be under the impression that having certain things, and being rich and successful will make them happy. (Of course those things may make them happy, but it's temporary. The feeling soon wears off.) That's what the adverts tell us and that's what most people believe. We only have to read the newspapers to see how false that assumption is. Happiness is elusive. The more we try to be happy, the less happy we'll be! These activities aim to show what happiness is all about. The Bible tells us that joy is what everyone is really searching for. Joy comes from knowing that God is in control of our lives. We can be joyful, even when we're facing major problems! The group members will have a chance to do street interviews, perform a sketchscript and check with a 'Happyometer' to find the true meaning of happiness.

Icebreaker (3 minutes)

You will need: an overhead projector acetate and pen (or a large sheet of paper and a felt pen) with the face illustrated below copied onto it in advance!

Display the picture to the group, and have a quick brainstorm in response to the question, 'How do you think this bloke feels?' At least one person should say that he is feeling happy! As the emotions are suggested (eg pleased, smug, excited, delighted etc) write them around the edge of the picture, or get a group member to. Briefly discuss how appearances can be deceptive – although he looks happy, he could just be putting a brave face on things and be really miserable inside. In the same way, people who are really happy don't necessarily go around with a big grin on their face! Outward appearance doesn't mean very much as far as happiness is concerned. So, if it's not about smiling all the time, what *is* happiness? Add any suggestions to the sheet. Explain that this session will help us find out more about happiness and how we can be really happy.

Icebreaker (10 minutes)

You will need: a cassette recorder and separate microphone, with recordings of well known songs about happiness for the group members to 'sing along' to, karaoke style. If you are stuck for suitable songs, ask your group members in advance. They will not only know some songs, but more than likely will be able to provide you with the cassettes (or records or CDs)! Two possibilities are: 'Happiness' sung by Ken Dodd (from his album *Ken Dodd: Great Hits*, available to order from record shops) or 'Don't Worry, Be Happy' sung by Bobby McFerrin (distributed by EMI on the *Simple Pleasures* album and also available to order). If you use either of these songs, do check with your group members first and make sure that they know them!

If you are not sure how karaoke should be organised, ask the group members. They will be able to tell you!

Activity (15 minutes)

You will need: several large sheets of paper, magazines, travel brochures, newspapers, scissors, glue and felt pens (enough for the whole group to make a collage, or several smaller groups to make one each).

Either in small groups, or with everyone together, explain to the group that they have, say, twelve minutes to make a collage in two parts, entitled 'Things that make us happy' and 'Things that make us sad'. When the time is up, look at the results together and then discuss the following questions:
1. When do you feel happiest? (Try to get the group to think beyond materialistic things to feelings, such as being loved, helping others, being forgiven etc.)
2. Does money, health or things that happen to us affect our happiness? If they do, do you think they should?

Bible search (12 minutes)

You will need: copies of the 'Are you happy?' sheets, Bibles and pencils (enough for one per group member)

Either get the group members to work individually or in small groups, depending on their ability and whether or not they are used to finding Bible references. The instructions are at the top of the 'Are you happy?' sheets. Give them a time limit of, say, ten minutes and possibly have a small prize for the first finished. (The answer is *Your presence fills me with joy, and brings me pleasure for ever*.)

Discussion questions (6 minutes)

Find Psalm 16:11 and get a group member to read it – does anyone recognise it as the verse they have just decoded? Ask the group:
- What does this verse mean? (Being with God brings joy and pleasure.)
- What is the difference between joy and happiness? (Happiness tends to depend on what happens to us, but joy goes deeper, and stays with us despite our circumstances.)
- How can we be joyful? (We can't make ourselves be joyful, it comes naturally when we ask God to be in control of our lives, because we know that he cares for us. Joy is a gift that God's Holy Spirit gives us – Galatians 5:22.)

Role-play (18 minutes)

You will need: a Bible atlas and Bibles.

To put this activity in context, ask the group members if any of them have ever been on holiday to Greece. Explain that Philippi was a town in northern Greece which Paul visited on one of his missionary journeys. Find it on a map. Afterwards, Paul wrote a 'thank you letter' from his prison cell to thank the people of Philippi for the way they had supported him.

Divide the group into pairs. (If there are odd numbers, perhaps you could join up with a group member who wouldn't find you too inhibiting!) Explain that they are both Philippians, one happy and the other sad. Paul's letter has just arrived. Ask them to work out a conversation in which the happy person tries to cheer up the sad one. Give them the following extracts from Paul's letter to refer to in their role-play: Philippians 1:1–6; 2:14–16; 4:4–9.

After about ten minutes, bring everyone back together and watch a few of the role plays. You could finish in the same way that Paul finished his letters, reading together Philippians 4:23, or by saying the Grace together.

Songs

Hallelujah! for the Lord our God the Almighty reigns (*Mission Praise* 65)
Jubilate ev'rybody (*Mission Praise* 130)
O give thanks to the Lord (*Mission Praise* 182)
Rejoice in the Lord always (*Mission Praise* 194)
Come on and celebrate (*Mission Praise* 330)
God is good, we sing and shout it (*Mission Praise* 370)
I am a new creation (*Mission Praise* 404)
Jesus put this song into our hearts (*Mission Praise* 457)
Rejoice! Rejoice! (*Mission Praise* 543)

Mime (10 minutes)

Read the Bible passage on 'True Happiness' to the group – Matthew 5:3–11, then divide the group into pairs (or threes if necessary). Give each pair a verse each and, say, four minutes to work out a mime to accompany their verse and bring out the meaning. It might be a good idea for you to add the word 'because' in between the first and second phrases of each verse, as this makes the meaning clearer. Explain to the group why you are adding the word 'because'. When the groups have worked out their mimes, sit the pairs in order around a large circle on the floor and then read the passage slowly (adding the word 'because') and pausing after each verse. As you read each verse, each pair could either stand up and mime where they are, or move into the centre of the circle. Finish with the whole group reading the first half of verse twelve together.

Activity (10 minutes)

You will need: a Happyometer! To make one, take a large circle of stiff card and attach centrally to it a pointer which stretches a complete diameter. The circle should be divided into six. In the top sector write 'Happiness and Pleasure': in the sector opposite write 'Keen on sport – music – humour – hobbies – jokes'. In the top left write 'Joy': in the sector opposite write a list which reflects the qualities listed in Galatians 5:22 (considerate, ready to serve etc). In the top right write 'Unhappiness': in the sector opposite write words indicating the complete opposite of Galatians 5:22.

Show the Happyometer to the group (giving it a big build-up!) and ask one of them to choose a word in the lower part of the dial which they think describes their character or interests, and get them to come and point the indicator to that word. The top of the pointer will then indicate whether or not this will give them happiness, joy or unhappiness. Explain to the group how some aspects of our character give us pleasure and happiness, while others (such as generosity) will produce something deeper – joy. Use some more volunteers to show how most people are a mixture of happiness and joy at different times and all of us experience unhappiness sometimes as well, when we are selfish or unkind, for example. Try the Happyometer on some famous people (such as Mother Teresa, Hitler, football stars, TV personalities, pop singers etc, as well as some biblical characters such as Moses, Peter and even Jesus).

Ask the group:
- Should a Christian be happy and/or joyful all the time? (We can aim to be – Jesus helps us to overcome the wrong attitudes we have, bit by bit. When we do make a mistake, he forgives us so that we can start again.)
- Finish by reading Galatians 5:22 together and pointing out that they are the qualities listed in the joy section of the Happyometer.

Activity (10 minutes)

The 'Happiness' funsheet is one for people to use at home.

Are you happy ?

All the references below are found in the book of Psalms.

The first number is the **chapter**, the second number is the **verse** and the number in brackets is the **word**, whose **first letter** is the one you need to write in the box beside the reference.

For example, 91:10 (4) is **D**.

When you have found each letter, spell out the sentences they make.

108:4 (1)	80:9 (17)	69:12 (11)	119:49 (1)	140:2 (4)	18:7 (12)	16:3 (2)	80:12 (15)	28:9 (20)	48:13 (2)	59:13 (8)	31:19 (14)	72:16 (18)	80:11 (3)	89:14 (9)	95:2 (1)	107:42 (3)	119:58 (6)	65:13 (13)	10:3 (2)	80:10 (6)	91:15 (9)	103:17 (5)	4:7 (3)	38:8 (4)	91:7 (7)

28:7 (4)	23:3 (4)	79:11 (19)	109:5 (4)	78:56 (3)	18:5 (12)	105:12 (6)	112:2 (2)	72:15 (15)	80:3 (9)	45:5 (11)	29:2 (1)	68:6 (4)	72:9 (12)	102:26 (10)	71:16 (6)	89:17 (3)	105:29 (4)	119:54 (4)	24:4 (17)	38:11 (11)	50:8 (4)	48:10 (6)	149:4 (13)	121:2 (12)	91:7 (11)

Happiness!

Did you know …?

The 2nd most frequent command in the bible is REJOICE! (It's there nearly 300 times.)

Jesus wants us to be happy. (See John 15:11.)

List here three things that make you happy.

....

....

....

Christians should be happy people (though you wouldn't think so the look at some!)

The Bible says, that being a Christian should fill us with JOY!

What about Mary?

When Mary became pregnant she faced being deserted by her fiancé and dropped by her family and friends, relying on begging as an unmarried mother. But she was happy! Why?

Look at Luke 1:46–55 (particularly verses 46–49)

Circumstances (what's happening to us) shouldn't affect how we feel about God. Why not?

Find 1 Thessalonians 5:16–18.

Highlight it in your Bible.

Learn it by heart.

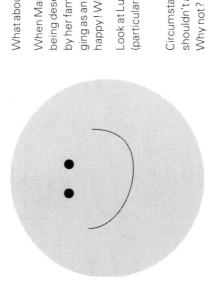

Game (12 minutes)

In advance, prepare a set of cards (plus duplicates, if you have a big group) as follows:

- Blind man
- Eyesight
- Millionaire
- Money
- Widow
- Husband
- Shopkeeper
- Customers
- Farmer
- Crops

You will also need four additional cards (marked with a 'B' on the back) with 'The joy that the Lord gives you will make you strong' (Nehemiah 8:10) written on them. (These will be used when the game is played a second time.) Mark the back of the cards in the left-hand column with an 'A', and the back of the cards in the right-hand column with a 'B'. To play the game, shuffle the cards and place them face down on a table or on the floor, in two rows of 'A' and 'B' cards. In turn, each player picks up two cards, one from each column. If the cards match correctly to make a pair, the player keeps them. If they don't match they need to be replaced, face down. The winner is the player with the most pairs. Explain that the 'A' cards represent people with needs and the 'B' cards represent what is normally required to bring temporary happiness. Now, reshuffle the cards and add the additional 'B' cards to the existing 'B' column. Play again with all the cards. Draw the group's attention to the fact that 'The joy that the Lord gives you will make you strong' means that people can still be satisfied even if they don't get what they want. (For example a widow may still have joy, in spite of her loneliness. Joy doesn't depend on getting what we want, but comes as the result of friendship with God.)

Bible focus (15 minutes)

You will need: Bibles, pens and pencils for everyone.

Ask the group to tell you what the opposite of happiness is, and then spend a few minutes discussing the things that might make us unhappy (such as circumstances like bereavement, loneliness etc). Explain how we can often be unhappy if our relationships have been spoilt. Again ask for examples (such as quarrels with friends, arguments at home etc). Often we can be unhappy because we are not forgiving somebody, or because they're not willing to forgive us. The Bible has a lot to say about forgiveness. Divide the group in half and give each half a question to answer together, with a set of references to help them.

1. What do we need to do if we need forgiveness – and what will God do? (1 John 1:9; Ephesians 1:7; Psalm 103:3.)
2. Why should we forgive others, even if we don't feel like it? (Luke 23:33,34; Matthew 18:21,22; Mark 11:25; Luke 6:37.)

Report back as a big group.

Activity (8 minutes)

Read the story of the unforgiving servant in dramatised form – Matthew 18:21–35. You will need the following parts: narrator, Peter, Jesus, King, Servant, Fellow-servant, and the rest of the group could have non-speaking parts and mime Jesus' disciples, a jailor and prison guards.

Outside activity

Why not get the group to do 'Vox Pop' street interviews to find out what the public think about happiness and how you can get it? You will need to accompany the group, who should go in pairs. The 'interviews' should be properly set up, with the group members having worked out a brief questionnaire beforehand and knowing the way in which the answers will be recorded. To create the right impression, the questions should be properly typed out on a sheet, and the interviewers equipped with clipboards and pens.

Obviously you will need to emphasise the importance of politeness. It's a good idea to give the unsuspecting interviewee an escape route. ('Would you like to answer a few simple questions for a survey we're doing, or haven't you got time at the moment?' might be a tactful approach!) It would be advisable to get written permission from parents before the group members are let loose on the unsuspecting public in your local area! Remind the group about road safety as well, and a phone call to the local police station to let them know what will be happening would also be a good idea! Suggestions for questions:

- What do you think makes people happy?
- Do you think most people in this country are happy?
- If the answer to the above question was no, why not?
- Do you think Christians are happy?

Outings

> Jesus said, 'I have come in order that you might have life – life in all its fullness' (John 10:10).

Read the above verse to the group. Jesus was referring to eternal life, which isn't just about heaven, and so ask the group how they think we could enjoy life to the full here and now as well. To start them thinking, suggest that they imagine that, when they get to heaven, God asks them if they have enjoyed the world he created for them. What about mountains, for example, or the sea? How could you encourage your group to enjoy them? Perhaps you could go and see (and even climb) some mountains, or visit the seaside (if you live in a part of the country where that's not too difficult!). Take a look at your local area. There must be things not too far away which God created, and which your group could enjoy to the full, together. Even in inner-city areas there are unexpected surprises – why not visit the local park or recreation ground? Other activities could include visits to a zoo or country park. Or how about a ramble, or bike ride? Ways of enjoying our God-given skills could include swimming, various sports activities (how about arranging matches with other groups?) organised team games, ten-pin bowling and ice-skating.

Videos

Harley Harley was a tough city kid. A holiday on a Texas ranch was the worst thing he could imagine, but it was there he found a purpose for life. (60 minutes - CRP)

In the Bin Arthur Stanley Grimble has a mask for every occasion and mood, until the dustman takes them away! (12 minutes – Scripture Union/CRP)

11. Hassle

Introduction

Most of your group members will be on the verge of adolescence, with all the agonies it will bring. The 'hassles' they will face, whether they be acne or bullying at school, will be major problems for them, and a cause of heartache and distress. Try and put yourself in their shoes – the activities suggested will help them face up to their problems and find ways of dealing with them from a Christian point of view. The Bible may not say anything about teenage spots, but it does show us how much God loves us just as we are. At an age when their self-esteem is easily knocked, the games, discussion questions and agony column 'phone-in' will help the group members realise that they *are* valuable to each other, to you, and to God.

Icebreaker (20 minutes)

You will need: a roll of lining paper (if you can't get that, a roll of old wallpaper would do, but be careful because it will tear easily!), some pencils, several pairs of scissors and thick felt pens of different colours.

You will need to know your group quite well before you attempt this activity and it will probably make you feel vulnerable yourself! If you can do it, it's a valuable way of talking about some of the group members' possible problems, without being too pointed!

Ask the group members to sit on the floor in a large circle. Unroll the paper to a length of about six feet, and secure the corners. Explain to the group that you are going to lie on it, and ask them to draw round your outline. When they have finished, get one or two of them to cut you out!

Secure the shape to the floor, get some group members to draw a face on it, then tell the group 'your story', using the outline given, as an example.

Be tactful, and adapt the story if necessary! Beware of any insensitive group members who giggle, or draw attention to others with the problems you're referring to.

Story outline

This is me *(point to yourself)*! And this is me when I was about your age *(point to the figure on the floor)* … not a very beautiful specimen really! For a start, I was very short-sighted, so I wore thick glasses *(draw them on the figure with a felt pen)* and I had loads of spots on my chin *(draw them in)*! My mum said it was just my age, but none of my friends seemed to have them, or they just had better concealing cream than I did. I used to get up half an hour early

to squeeze them all before I went to school, as well as allowing time for my daily hair wash – my hair was more greasy than a fish and chip shop! *(Draw in some hair, or get a group member to.)* It was hardly surprising that I was the only one without a boyfriend/girlfriend. Valentine's day was the worst. No one believed my story about having moved recently, so my admirer's card would have been sent to the wrong address. I was very self-conscious and the slightest thing would make me blush *(draw red circles on the figure's cheeks)*. I didn't just go red – I mean people would try to post letters in my mouth. That's why the school bully picked on me – he/she knew I was an easy target. I thought it was the punch on the jaw he/she'd given me which had caused my toothache, but when it didn't go away and my mum forced me to go to the dentist, well that was BAD news! I got fixed up for a brace, with a load of wire in my mouth that made me look like Euston station. Aaaagh! *(Draw braces in.)* Even if I had been able to afford all the right gear, it would have looked ridiculous on me, but it might have helped. I suppose that being good at sport would have made a difference … no chance! Nobody wanted an overweight midget on the team. It would have been nice to be 'in' though.

When you have finished your story, tell the group members to put their hankies away and see if they can identify all the problems (hassles) you had at their age (short-sightedness, spots, greasy hair, no boyfriend/girlfriend, self-consciousness, victim of bullying, braces, unfashionable, overweight and too short.) As they mention each one, write it on the outline.

Finish with some comments along the following lines:

I suppose I was 'just the age' for those sorts of problems, and I did grow out of them eventually! Most of you are coming up to 'just the age' for all this *(indicate the outline figure on the floor)*, so life might be tough for a while. **You have been warned!** But cheer up – it won't last forever. Everybody goes through hassles like these at some stage when they're growing up, and they've survived them! So … be prepared – it won't be such of a shock to the system if you are!

What's really on your mind?

Appearance/street cred:

....

Health:

....

Boyfriends/girlfriends:

....

The future:

....

School and work:

....

God:

....

Family problems:

....

Money and things:

....

Sex:

....

Other:

....

Activity (15 minutes)

You will need: letters from the problem pages of teen magazines, cut out (*without* the answers!) and mounted on numbered cards, and enough pencils and photocopies of the 'What's *really* on your mind?' sheets for each group member.

Place the problem letter cards round the room and ask the group members to work in twos or threes. Give them the sheets and pencils and ask them to read each letter and decide what it is that the writer is *really* worried about. Explain that this might be more obvious in some letters than others. Each letter needs to be placed in one of the categories mentioned on the sheet, by writing the appropriate number next to that category.

After, say, five minutes, bring everyone together and compare results. Did all the groups reach the same conclusions? Were most of the letter writers worried about the same things? What were they most worried and least worried about? You could re-order the list on the sheet to make a 'top ten' of hassles. If appropriate, give the group members a few minutes to think about their own hassles before you pray a prayer on their behalf, along the following lines:

> *Father God, you know the hassles that we have at the moment, especially … and … Please help us know the best way to cope with these problems.*

Explain to the group that the other activities may help them find some possible answers to their hassles and that if they want to talk privately and confidentially about anything, you (or a suitable counsellor) would be very happy to listen.

Bible focus (15 minutes)

You will need: Bibles, pens, and an overhead projector acetate or sheet of paper with the paraphrase of the passage (complete with blanks, as given below) copied onto it.

Explain to the group that they are going to find out what the Bible says about our worries and hassles. Read Matthew 6:25–34 (which shows how Jesus understood that his followers sometimes got hassled) with the group and then divide them into three and ask each small group to answer the following questions:
1. What things are we told not to worry about?
2. Can you find three reasons why we need not worry?
3. What is worth worrying about?
After three or four minutes get each small group to report back. Get everyone together, show the group the paraphrase of the passage, and ask them to fill in the blanks so as to make the passage refer to their specific needs. (Eg Jesus says, 'Don't worry about street-cred because …' etc.)

> Jesus says, 'Don't worry about … because … is more important than … God even looks after birds and you are much more … than they are. Anyway, worrying doesn't … Instead, concentrate on … and God will …

Activity (20 minutes)

You will need: Bibles, pencils and paper, a telephone and tables and chairs arranged for a 'phone-in' with the four people who will be phoning in sitting facing the four people who will be answering their calls. A 'presenter' could sit between the two tables, and any extra group members be seated to form an audience. (The diagram might help!)

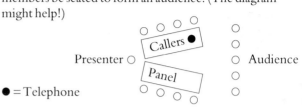

Explain to the group that they are going to produce an imaginary radio 'phone-in' programme. Divide them into four groups, and give each group one of the 'scripts' (copied from the selection given, or adapted as appropriate). Allow them, say, ten minutes to examine together the problem outlined in the script and discuss the most helpful answer to give. Encourage them to prepare their answers from a Christian point of view and to use any of the Bible verses given with the scripts, if appropriate. When they've done this they will need to choose a person to 'ring in' with the problem, and someone to answer them, who will sit on the panel in the 'recording studio'!

Set up the 'live recording' with the group members seated according to their role. Either present the programme yourself, or choose a suitable group member to keep it moving! In turn, the four selected group members use the phone to 'ring in' with their problem (they can use the script) and the appropriate person gives advice 'on air' (they can use notes if they need to!). After each problem, the presenter could invite further comments or advice from the studio audience.

Scripts for the 'phone-in':

> Do you think I'll ever get a job when I leave school? My big brother left school two years ago and he's never got a job. Sometimes I lie awake at night worrying about it. Do you think I'm stupid?

> My parents are always arguing and fighting. Last Friday they had a huge row and my dad said, 'That's the last straw.' He went out and didn't come back till Monday. They're going to get a divorce and I think it's my fault. What can I do to keep them together? Should I leave home? I am fifteen.

> Last year I moved to a new school. Some of the kids in my class are OK but there is one who is always picking on me. He calls me names, tells jokes about me and pushes me around in the corridors. Now some of his friends have started doing it as well. I can't say anything to the teachers or he will kill me. What shall I do?

> I've been invited to my best friend's party next week. I want to go but I can't because everyone is buying new clothes for it and I haven't got any money. Should I tell her I've been grounded?

Helpful Bible verses:
- 'Don't be afraid or discouraged, for I, the LORD your God, am with you wherever you go' (Joshua 1:9).
- 'I alone know the plans I have for you ... plans to bring about the future you hope for' (Jeremiah 29:11).
- 'Don't worry about anything, but in all your prayers ask God for what you need, always asking him with a thankful heart' (Philippians 4:6).
- 'God's peace, which is far beyond human understanding, will keep your hearts and minds safe' (Philippians 4:7).
- 'My God will supply all your needs' (Philippians 4:19).
- 'Leave all your worries with him, because he cares for you' (1 Peter 5:7).

Activity (15 minutes)

You will need: clay or Plasticine, and pipe cleaners (enough for, say, at least eight per person), paper and felt pens.

Start by asking the group if they can think of an old proverb about sharing problems (such as 'A problem shared is a problem halved'). Explain that a similar proverb in the Bible talks about problems and hassles as 'burdens'. Read Galatians 6:2.

Provide the group members with the medium of their choice and give them, say, ten minutes, to create a model or picture which illustrates the idea of 'carrying each other's burdens'. Emphasise that you are not looking for artistic masterpieces, just something to illustrate the *idea*. They can either work on their own or in pairs. When the time is up, get them to show the rest of the group their creation! Make sure you say something affirming about each one and don't let the group members laugh at each other's efforts.

Suggest that after the meeting the group members make it a priority to find someone to share their problems with. It may be a group member, or another friend outside the group. Encourage them to talk to a Christian about their problems, and emphasise that you would be happy to listen if they wanted to talk to you at any time. You could symbolise the mutual support which the group offers by joining all the artistic creations together (which may only be possible if everyone has used pipe cleaners!).

Discussion questions (20 minutes)

Read out the extract below.

Bullying

Britain needs a national initiative on bullying, requiring each school to have a written policy, according to the national charity *Childline*. They analysed over 2,000 calls received and concluded that 'it is quite clear that bullying is not a trivial problem' according to Esther Rantzen, chair of *Childline*. A quarter of reported bullying involved violence, some of it resulting in severe damage. Half of the callers had suffered continued bullying over many months. Children over 13, especially boys, it is suggested, are often encouraged to feel that they must deal with the situation themselves. In two-thirds of cases where adults tried to help, the bullying stopped.
– from *Young People Now* magazine

Open a discussion using some of these questions:
- Would you agree with Esther Rantzen that ' ... bullying is not a trivial problem'? Why?
- Have any of you ever been victims of bullying?
- If not, do you know people who have?
- If so, what did you or they do about it?
- What advice would you give to a first year at school who was being bullied?

Finish by reading the group Chapter 4 from *The Chocolate Teapot*, by David Lawrence (published by Scripture Union), which is all about being bullied, and puts the problem in a biblical perspective.

Activity (8 minutes)

You will need: enough small stones or pieces of gravel for everyone!

If your group members know each other quite well and would respond sensitively to this activity, they might be prepared to do a bit of practical 'burden sharing'. If you do not have even numbers you will need to be prepared to pair up with a group member who could cope with you!

Give each group member a stone and then ask them to get into twos. Tell them to think of one hassle they have at the moment which they could share with their partner. Ask them to imagine that the stone represents their worry and to explain it briefly in for example the following way: 'This stone is the exam I've got next week which I think I'm going to fail,' or, 'This stone represents my brother who's ill in hospital.' If the partner is willing to share the 'burden' they take the stone and put it down the inside of their shoe. When this is done, they swop over and the other person shares their 'burden'.

Suggest to the group members that they keep the stone in their shoe for at least the rest of the day. Each time they feel it, they could pray about their partner's problem.

Prayer (10 minutes)

Suggest that the group members sit in a space and close their eyes so that they are not distracted. Ask them to imagine that they are the only person in the room – just them and God, who loves them very much and cares about the things they care about. Explain that you will play some music for them to listen to and they could use the time to tell God about their hassles. They might like to think of one specific thing that's worrying them, and hand it over to God.

60 Play some suitable music. Instrumental music or Christian worship tapes would be appropriate. You might also like to read some Bible verses (perhaps Psalm 30 or 31), or the words from Christian choruses.

You could finish by playing a song such as 'Why worry' by Dire Straits, from the album *Brothers in arms*, or 'I will always love you' by Jo King, from the album *Straight from the heart*. At the end of the song close with a short prayer, offering all our hassles to God.

Visiting speakers

Why not invite someone from a counselling agency to talk to the group and answer questions about their work? You could ask them to mention the sorts of problems they deal with, how they go about helping people and what ideas they have for coping with problems and stress. If possible, ask them to talk about the importance of listening when helping people with problems – perhaps they could demonstrate some basic listening skills and help the group to practise

them. As counselling agencies often rely on voluntary funding, they would welcome any support your group could give. A sponsored silence might be an appropriate way of raising money for them!

Or, how about inviting a Christian who has just left school to visit the group and talk about how they coped with hassles at school, and whether being a Christian made it easier.

Songs

Father, I place into your hands (*Mission Praise* 45)
I will call upon the Lord (*Mission Praise* 96)
Jesus take me as I am (*Mission Praise* 127)
What a friend we have in Jesus (*Mission Praise* 262)
Be bold, be strong, for the Lord your God is with you
    (*Mission Praise* 312)
He that is in us is greater (*Mission Praise* 388)
Lord, in my anxiety

Lord, in my anxiety © Peter Graystone *Tune: traditional Canadian*

* From verse 2 onward repeat these two bars in cumulative fashion, starting with the last verse you sang and working your way back to 'the love of God'.
(The simplest way to describe this is by comparing it with 'One man went to mow'.)

12. Leisure

Introduction

Ever heard of celebrating Christmas in the middle of summer? That's one of the suggestions in this material! The aim is to help the group members look at their leisure time (including holidays and the celebration of festivals, which is where Christmas comes in) from a Christian point of view. There are plenty of ways for your group to get to know each other better. One of the ideas is that they plan and put together a programme of social activities such as swimming, ten-pin bowling or ice-skating … so make sure you're ready for action!

Icebreaker (20 minutes)

You will need: blank overhead projector acetates and pens (or large sheets of paper and felt pens) and pencils and paper for each small group.

Divide the group into threes or fours. Give each group ten minutes to design their own theme park. They need to consider what the overall theme would be; what the star attraction would be; how many different rides or activities would be related to the theme; what menus they would offer in the restaurants, burger bars, ice-cream shops etc, to fit in with their theme. Encourage them to draw maps and sketches and to give their theme park a name.

Now give each small group two or three minutes to 'sell' their theme park to the rest of the group, using the overhead projector if they need to. This could be done in the style of an advert.

Activity (20 minutes)

Don't just talk about leisure, but arrange some leisure activities you can do together as a group. First of all, review your programme with the members to see what proportion of time is spent on, for example:
- Specifically Christian activities like worship and Bible study.
- Recreational or social activities.
- Activities which help others.

Together draw up a programme for the next two or three months to include these elements. (For ideas, see the suggestions below.) When the programme has been planned, why not get one or two artistic group members to design it, and then photocopy one for each person?

- Ask each group member to bring to the next meeting one book, one magazine and one piece of music that they enjoy. Give each person a brief time to share what they have brought and say why they like it.
- How about organising an art exhibition, brass rubbing, a computer games evening, a cycling trip, a DIY concert, a photographic competition, carol singing, rambles, a sports day, a swimming outing, or a treasure hunt? Or perhaps you could make your own video programme, visit the beach, go to the cinema or a disco, take in the ice rink, leisure centre, museum, theatre or even theme park! There are plenty of suggestions to be getting on with!
- Remember to include activities which help others. Some of the above suggestions could be adapted to do this, for example the diy concert could be performed in a local old people's home.

Game (15 minutes)

Ask each group member to bring one or two picture postcards of holiday resorts. Spread them out around the room and ask everyone to identify as many places as they can.

Get them to share their holiday experiences, either spontaneously or by being interviewed. What did they enjoy most about the holiday? What did they do each day?

Activity (20 minutes)

As a group, watch some Christian music videos, or play some Christian tapes or CDs. Get group members to bring their favourites and say why they like them. Discuss their quality and content. Do they offer anything that secular tapes don't? What does secular music offer that Christian music doesn't? If you have musical talent in the group, have a go at writing and performing your own song – Christian or secular – and recording or videoing it.

Survey (10 minutes)

You will need: photocopies of the 'Fun and games' survey.

Giving a time limit of, say, eight minutes, use the surveys to allow group members to find out about one other person's leisure interests. When they have all finished their sheets, come together to discuss the findings. Taking a vote on the most popular leisure interests could be fun.

Story (5 minutes)

The Jester

The Jester sits in the corner and chatters continually. The King hired him originally to help him relax when his mind was troubled with affairs of state. In the beginning the King would bid him be quiet when he'd heard enough, but soon it became easier to listen to the fool's madness than to think about running the country, so now he lets him ramble on – sometimes he listens, sometimes he doesn't.

Occasionally the fool says something which everyone considers to be wise, so the king lets his children come and listen to him. The Queen often dumps them in front of him when they're getting under her feet. She thinks it a harmless way of occupying them, although the Jester does tell some rather bawdy stories, and the servants say that the children are showing signs of becoming more like him than their mother and father.

The Queen likes to listen to the Jester with her husband – it's something they can do together; she likes the fool because he's always up to date with the latest news and gossip, and because he tells such romantic stories. Being of royal blood she is of delicate sensibility, and when the fool first came she was often shocked by some of the dreadful things he would suddenly come out with (the trouble is that because of his madness you never know what he's going to say next). With time, however, she found these outbursts less and less objectionable. Now she is rarely shocked or offended.

There are many improvements the Royal Family would like to see made in their kingdom, but the Jester's ramblings keep them from dwelling on these overmuch, and besides – nowadays they never seem to have the time …

Discussion questions

After you have read the story, ask the group members if they have worked out the riddle. Who or what is 'The Jester'? (Answer: the television!) Do the group members agree with the point of the story? Are they like the King and Queen, letting the Jester ramble on all day, taking up too much of their time?

Outside activity

Invite the group to your home, or go to a group member's home so that you can all watch a selected television together. (Suitable programmes would be soap operas, which most of the group will be familiar with anyway, or a 'sit-com' or regular series.)

Hand out paper and pencils and explain that you want them to think about the following questions:

1. Is the programme unnecessarily violent?
2. Is there a lot of bad language?
3. Are there any obscene or blasphemous words? (You may need to explain what the difference is between bad language, obscenity and blasphemy.)
4. Is the overall effect of the programme likely to be helpful or unhelpful?
5. What was good about the programme?

Afterwards, discuss the observations the group made and consider sending a letter of appreciation or criticism (or both) to the appropriate TV authority, explaining the nature of your group and why you watched the programme together. Write to: The Independent Broadcasting Authority, 70 Brompton Road, London SW3 1EY, or The BBC, Broadcasting House, London W1A 1AA.

Finish by praying for any Christians you know who work in the media, and for TV producers and writers.

Bible focus (20 minutes)

You will need: Bibles, different coloured felt pens, pencils, paper, glue, scissors, a scrapbook, Bible encyclopaedias and reference books (suitable ones include *Look into the Bible* published by Scripture Union and *Encyclopaedia of the Bible* and *Handbook to the Bible*, both published by Lion Publishing) and a cassette recorder and blank cassette.

Read Leviticus 23:1–4 to the group and then divide the group into twos and threes and give each small group one of the following sections from the rest of the chapter: verses 5–14 (Passover and Unleavened Bread), verses 15–22 (Harvest), verses 23–25 (New Year), verses 26–32 (Day of Atonement), verses 33–44 (Festival of Shelters). Give the groups, say, fifteen minutes to produce a short account of their particular festival for the scrapbook. They need to say what the festival celebrates and what happens during it. This could be presented in a number of ways:

- From a journalist's point of view as a newspaper article.
- Group members could imagine that they were there and prepare (as a small group or individually) some holiday photos with captions.
- The accounts could take the form of postcards or letters to a friend.
- If you have group members who hate writing, why not give them a cassette recorder to record a radio-style report, or a telephone so that they could work out a sketch in which they have a phone conversation with a friend or relative?

When the time is up, get each group to present their accounts and then stick them in the scrapbook.

Activity (20 minutes)

You will need: Bibles and an overhead projector acetate and pen or a large sheet of paper and a felt pen.

Brainstorm with the group and list as many Christian festivals and special days of thanksgiving as possible, writing them in a column on the sheet. Add any from the list below which the group have not mentioned, explaining what the more obscure ones (eg Rogation) are about. Explain that some churches celebrate all the festivals listed while others only celebrate a few, but that all Christians all over the world celebrate Christmas and Easter, which are central to the Christian faith. Ask the group to number the festivals in order through the Christian year, starting with the promised birth of Jesus. Christian festivals/special days of prayer and thanksgiving (and what we remember or celebrate) include:

- Advent (The coming of Jesus)
- Christmas (The birth of Jesus)
- Epiphany (The wise men visit Jesus)
- Lent (The time when Jesus was in the wilderness, being tempted by the devil)
- Palm Sunday (Jesus' triumphant entry into Jerusalem)
- Maundy Thursday (The first celebration of the Lord's Supper, or Holy Communion)
- Good Friday (The crucifixion of Jesus)
- Easter Sunday (Jesus rises from the dead)
- Ascension day (Jesus ascends to heaven)
- Pentecost [or Whitsun] (The coming of God's Holy Spirit)
- Rogation (God's blessing of the crops)
- Harvest (Thanksgiving for gathering in the crops)

You could mention that our word 'holiday' derives from 'holy days', and discuss how we might learn to appreciate more deeply the spiritual significance of some of our holidays.

Meditation (15 minutes)

Give some group members (preferably the good readers) the following Bible passages and verses from songs. Explain to the group that they will have a chance to focus on the fact that Jesus was born to live, die and rise again. Suggest that they read their verses in the order shown, with a pause for silent prayer between each section.

- Read Luke 2:1–7
  Read the first two verses of 'Once in Royal David's City' (*Mission Praise* 530)

  Pause

- Read Matthew 27:27–31
  Read the first two verses of 'There is a green hill far away' (*Mission Praise* 230)

  Pause

- Read Matthew 28:1–8
  Read (or sing this time) the first verse and chorus of 'In the tomb so cold they laid him' (*Mission Praise* 438)

Activity

Why not celebrate Christmas at one of your meetings during the middle of summer? After all, it's because of Jesus' birthday that your group exists! Concentrate on the Christian aspects of the festival rather than all the other traditions. You could have a party with refreshments and carol singing and maybe the group could make cards to give to each other. (Just an idea!)

Prayer (20 minutes)

Have a selection of newspapers or magazines available. Pin up some large sheets of paper headed PRAISE, PEOPLE and PROBLEMS. Cut from the newspapers and magazines pictures and words which show aspects of leisure for which we can praise God (eg man-made facilities, the natural world, our bodies etc); people in the leisure industry (sports personalities, pop stars etc) who need our prayers; and any pictures which show the problems of leisure (lack of facilities in a particular area, gambling addiction, apathy etc). Stick these up under the appropriate headings. Use the result as inspiration for a series of spontaneous, one sentence prayers from the group, prayed with eyes open as they stand looking at the pictures.

Worship

Explain that the group can thank God for, and celebrate, leisure and creativity. Discuss how the leisure activities we take part in, such as sport or music, are an expression of ourselves and, as such, can be 'worship' – acknowledging God and giving ourselves and our abilities to him. (Refer to Romans 12:1.)

Together, compile an act of worship which uses the gifts of the group – whatever they may be – and reflects and uses their interests and activities. If the group is keen on outdoor activities, worship in the open air; for a TV orientated group, use a video (like *Stop and Think* – see below) in worship. Group members with musical skills might be able to lead some singing. Budding actors could perform a dramatised Bible story.

Book suggestions

Hawkeye Hits the Jackpot (Veronica Heley, published by Scripture Union) is a story about gaming machines.
Don't Call Me Chicken (Peggy Burns, published by Harvestime) is about video nasties.
Walking Disaster (Gail Vinall, published by Scripture Union) is about a group of hikers doing the 'Ten Tors' across Dartmoor.
All of these could be used as serial stories, or you could encourage group members to read them in their own time and then discuss them.

Videos

McGee and me – The Not So Great Escape Nicholas wants to watch the horror movie all his friends are watching … (30 minutes – CRP)
Amazing Escapes of Mr Gilbert Escapologist Pete Gilbert is locked in a barrel of water and hung in a straight-jacket, but he still finds time to talk about his faith! (20 minutes – CRP)
A Sports Odyssey Surfing, skiing, water-skiing, hang-gliding, skateboarding and motorcycling – spectacular photography and Christian testimonies from some of the stars. (40 minutes – CRP)
Hoddle A documentary about the famous footballer in which he talks about his Christian faith. (40 minutes – CRP)
Stop and Think Five programmes intended for use in worship sessions (20 minutes per programme – CRP)

Fun and games survey

1. How much time per day in hours or minutes do you spend on the following activities?

.... Eating

.... Sleeping

.... Watching TV

.... Scratching your head

.... Walking the dog

2. Would you rather be ... ?

☐ a professional footballer

☐ an amateur gardener

☐ a daredevil hang-glider

☐ asleep

3. Does watching 'Neighbours' give you the same sense of excitement as ... ?

☐ eating cold custard

☐ climbing Everest

☐ watching 'Eastenders'

☐ sleeping

4. If you could invent a totally new leisure activity, what would it be?

....

5. If you could choose anything you liked to eat, what would it be?

....

6. Who is the ...

sportsperson you most admire?

....

pop star you most admire?

....

TV personality you most admire?

....

7. What is the best ...

book you have ever read?

....

play you have ever seen?

....

film you have ever seen?

....

TV programme you have ever watched?

....

8. Which out of these pairs of activities do you prefer?

Watching sport	☐	☐	or playing sport
Reading a book	☐	☐	or watching TV
Cycling	☐	☐	or swimming
Eating	☐	☐	or sleeping
Collecting things	☐	☐	or making things.

13. Love and sex

Introduction

The main aim of this material is to help the group members understand the real meaning of one of the most devalued words in our society. Love can mean so many different things, and there's so much more to it than a nice feeling, or sex, or red roses and romance. We are going to take a close look at the nitty-gritty of selfless Christian love and how we can apply the high standards of the Bible to all our relationships, not only to those with members of the opposite sex. *The Four Loves* by CS Lewis (published by Collins) identifies four different types of loving: affection (particularly family love), friendship, eros (the love between people 'in love') and charity (the love described by Paul in 1 Corinthians 13). As the group look at these different aspects of love we hope it will help them to form the right attitudes as a basis for all their relationships. After all, they're approaching those stormy teenage years, with all the agony and ecstasy of falling in and out of love, making lifelong friends of both sexes and, we hope, learning about the servant-like, sacrificial love which Jesus demonstrated.

Icebreaker (10 minutes)

You will need: a large outline drawing of a sundae dish on a sheet of paper, or in chalk on the floor, as well as different coloured felt-pens and small pieces of paper cut into exotic shapes to represent fruit, jelly, ice-cream, cream, wafers, chocolate flakes, sauce toppings etc … is your mouth watering yet?

Show the group the dish and explain that love can be a bit like an ice-cream sundae – a mixture of lots of different ingredients! Some mouthfuls taste heavenly, some ingredients can make it all go wrong; it can be just right, or it can be too sloppy; it can build us up, or it can do us harm.

Ask the group members to write different ingredients of love on the paper shapes and add them to the sundae dish. To help them get started, you could begin by adding pieces of paper with words such as caring, friendship, fun etc. …

When everyone has had a turn and the dish is full, look at the ingredients and discuss them. Have a lot of people added kindness? Do they think that patience has anything to do with love? If the four different loves mentioned by CS Lewis – affection, friendship, being 'in love' (eros) and charitable love (charity) – have not been included, you could add them to the sundae dish, briefly explaining each type as you do.

Activity (10 minutes)

Point out to the group that part of the problem is that the word 'love' can mean so many different things. Give the following statements as examples of this. You could display them on an overhead projector acetate or large sheet of paper. Divide the group into pairs and get them to say each statement to each other (with appropriate expression) and then work out what they *really* mean:

'I love Big Macs' *(means: The taste, aroma and texture of a burger really satisfy me!)*

'I love swimming' *(means: I really enjoy swimming – it gives me a lot of pleasure.)*

'I love my mum' *(means: We share a deep bond of affection loyalty and togetherness.)*

'I love you, my love, my dove, my angel, my sweetheart …' (Tell the group members very seriously that you expect them to say this with a straight face and without a giggle! – *it means: You make me feel happy and complete and I want to commit myself to you for the rest of my life … or: You make my knees turn to jelly, my heart flutter and my stomach churn.)*

Ask the various pairs to explain the real meaning of each phrase, and point out again that the word 'love' can mean so many different things. Finally (and you may prefer to tell your group this, rather than ask them the question) ask what the phrase 'a couple made love' means. You will probably get the answer, 'They had sex together.' That is correct, because that is what that phrase has come to mean, but point out to the group that, strictly speaking, it's not a true statement.

- It's impossible to 'make' love – sex doesn't 'make' it.
- Sex was designed for pleasure and reproduction, but having sex with someone doesn't make you love them.
- Sex with someone you love and are committed to in a marriage relationship is a way of *expressing* that love and commitment, and can bring you closer together.

You may like to invite a suitable visiting speaker, such as a Christian youth leader, doctor, or your local minister, to speak to the group about sex and love and answer their questions. (Obviously it would need to be someone known to you, who would not be easily shocked by frank questions and, most important of all, be on the wavelength of the group members. If they could be present for the whole of this session, before answering questions at the end, the ice could be broken and the question time be more relaxed.)

Songs

Father, we love you (*Mission Praise* 46)
Let there be love shared among us (*Mission Praise* 137)
A new commandment I give unto you (*Mission Praise* 283)
Come on and celebrate (*Mission Praise* 330)
From heaven you came, helpless babe (*Mission Praise* 361)
God is good, we sing and shout it (*Mission Praise* 370)
I'm special because God has loved me (*Mission Praise* 431)

Bible focus (15 minutes)

You will need: Bibles, pens and paper for each group member, and the following Bible references copied onto slips of paper: 1 Corinthians 6:12–14; Proverbs 6:20–32; Proverbs 7:6–27; Proverbs 5:15–20; Genesis 28:3; Hebrews 13:4.

Introduce this with a quick-fire game of word associations. You say a word to the group and the group member you point at has to say the first word that comes into their head in response. (Eg love – nice – sex – babies – pregnant – sex – marriage – bed – together –sex – love – fun – sex – AIDS – sex – love – God etc.) The repetitions are intentional – by leading the word-play you can keep it on the theme of sex!

Divide the group into threes and fours and give each small group a slip of paper with one of the Bible references on. Give them say, seven minutes to find their verses and then be ready to report back on what the Bible says about sex. Get each small group to summarise their verses and see if they can identify what God thinks about sex and marriage.

Ask the group what other reasons there are for not having sex outside marriage. (Examples could include the risk of AIDS, venereal disease, cervical cancer and unwanted pregnancies, which might then lead to abortion, 'shot-gun' weddings and illegitimate children.)

Discussion (20 minutes)

Read the following statements to the group:
• 'Haven't you done it yet? You're just a kid!'
• 'Don't worry, you can't get pregnant the first time.' (Not true)
• 'Go nearly all the way but stop in time, and you won't get pregnant.' (Not true)
• 'We did it twice last night. It was really good.'
Ask them if they ever hear this sort of thing said at school, or if any of their older friends have had sex. (The answer will probably be yes.) Point out that two of the statements aren't true.

Ask the group what they think they would do if they were pressurised to have sex with their regular boyfriend or girlfriend, or even if they found themselves in a situation that had got out of control, where it was difficult to stop (perhaps at a party and if they had had some alcohol, which would impair their judgment). Try not to be shocked at the things they might say, and make it clear that you appreciate that sexual feelings are very strong and that they can get 'turned on' very easily – especially boys. You will have to be prepared to be frank and honest! If you are, it will help the group members to think through this issue *before* they are confronted with it when they are a bit older.

Activity (10 minutes)

You will need: a large sheet of paper and felt pens. Either draw a few bricks on the paper in advance, or even get hold of a length of brick-style wallpaper to make a 'Graffiti Wall'. (Toy shops sell sheets of paper which look like brick walls, for use on dolls' houses. They're ideal and not expensive!)

Ask the group if they can think of a couple they know who have been happily married for a while. If they asked them if they loved each other, what answer do they think they would get? If they asked them if they felt 'head-over-heels' in love all the time, what do they think the answer would be? Now have a quick brainstorm on 'Real Love'. Get group members to scribble the suggestions on the graffiti wall. Here are a few ideas if they are stuck:

Real love …
• is what you do for someone, not just how you feel about them.
• lasts when you're apart – and sometimes grows even stronger!
• doesn't give up, even when things get tough.
• is being the first to say sorry.
• means carrying on loving someone even when you don't feel like it!

(You could also add quotes, poems and Bible verses to the wall.) To finish this activity, read the marriage vows from the marriage service – borrow a copy from your vicar or minister. Point out that the couple are asked, '*Will* you love each other?' not, '*Do* you love each other?' (Or see if the group spot that after you have read through the vows!) Marriage is all about an act of will (commitment) and not about feelings, which can come and go.

Outside activity

Why not interview some real people about their relationships? If you know of a suitable married couple from your church, for example, ask them if they would be prepared to be interviewed, and have the group as guests in their home for the occasion? Your group could offer to provide the refreshments!

Prepare the questions beforehand with the group. Here are some guidelines:
• How long have you been married?
• What made you decide to get married?
• Do you learn about relationships during marriage, or did you get everything right to start with?
• How would you describe your first year of marriage?
• Are good looks as important as a good character?
• Would you agree with the statement 'Marriage isn't a question of "give and take" – it's all give'?
• Do you argue?
• Do your feelings for each other change?
• What makes your marriage work?
• Would you say marriage was easy, or difficult? Why?
Arrange for different group members to ask each question. After your visit, perhaps they could all sign a 'Thank you' card for the couple.

Activity (20 minutes)

The 'Boy meets girl/girl meets boy' sheet can be used individually in the group time or at home.

Answers to the word search

```
L Y H T R O W T S U R T
U O N G E N E R O U S H
F E E V I T R O P P U S
H C O R I N L O Y A L I
T N T H I A O N H S K F
I U T H I R V T O I E L
A F F E C T I O N A T E
F E N V S F N D E O U S
R C A R I N G T S O S N
G N I V I G E V T E N U
```

Role-play (8 minutes)

This is a short, light-hearted activity, which would follow on well from the 'Boy meets girl/girl meets boy' sheet. You will need to decide whether or not your group can handle it. If they are the sort of group who would hate it, and end up feeling silly and embarrassed, then forget it!

Divide the group into pairs (you may need to pair up with someone yourself if there are odd numbers, so make sure your partner can cope with you!). If possible, there should be a boy and girl in each pair. If not, ask the groups of the same sex to decide who will take the part of the boy, and who will play the girl. It will help the atmosphere to be light-hearted if you name the pairs something like Arnold and Gertrude.

Explain to the pairs that their task is for the boy to ask the girl to go to the cinema with him to see (name the latest hit film that the group members would be 'into'). He has to ask in the following ways: confidently, timidly, aggressively, nervously, and cooly'! When the pairs have done this, ask one or two pairs to demonstrate their best role-play of the five to the other groups members, who need to try and guess the manner of asking.

Videos

Number One A telling cartoon story, which examines our relationships with other people and with God.
(17 minutes – Scripture Union/CRP)

O'Shea The story of Hosea's love for his wife, brilliantly told in a modern day setting.
(13 minutes – Scripture Union/CRP)

Let's Talk About Love Although this is not specifically Christian, this mixture of drama and interviews presents some of the facts about sex outside marriage and encourages teenagers to see sexual relationships within the context of a loving marriage. (25 minutes – CRP)

Activity (10 minutes)

You will need: copies of teen magazines and Bibles. The group members may be willing to lend their own copies of popular teenage magazines for this session! Examples could include: *Smash Hits* (a best selling pop magazine), *Fast Forward* (a weekly TV-orientated mag), *Just Seventeen* (a weekly, read by 11–15 year olds, despite its name. About 20% of its content deals with sex and its advice column is based on a secular humanistic world view) and *Mizz* (a fortnightly leading competitor to *Just Seventeen*).

Ask the group members to select extracts from these magazines that say anything about love. They may well come up with lyrics from pop songs, or snippets from articles or advice columns. They will use these extracts later. (Group members may need to share the magazines, but try to have enough for one between two.)

Now ask the group members to contrast the world's view of love with God's love. Get them each to find one of the following Bible references, and keep a marker in them, ready for reading out later:

> Deuteronomy 11:1; Psalm 23:6; Psalm 100:5;
> Psalm 108:4; Matthew 5:44; Luke 10:27;
> John 13:34; John 14:15; John 15:13; Romans 5:8;
> Romans 12:9; Romans 12:10;
> 1 Corinthians 13:4–8 (if you have a large group, this could be split into five separate verses);
> 1 Peter 3:8; 1 John 2:15; 1 John 4:16.

When all the group are ready, ask each member in turn to read the magazine extract, followed by the Bible verse about God's love. Finish by reading 1 John 3:16, explaining it briefly if appropriate.

Activity (20 minutes)

You will need: a Bible, some washing up bowls full of warm water, soap and towels, and plastic sheeting for the floor (dustbin bags would do).

Remind the group of Jesus' love, which meant he died on the cross to take the punishment for our sin instead of us. Explain that you are not only going to find out more about the way Jesus showed his love for others, you are all going to demonstrate it!

Read John 13:3–9 to the group and divide them into pairs. Explain that they are going to do what Jesus did, and serve each other by washing each other's feet. When each pair has a bowl, a towel and some soap, they can take it in turns to wash and dry their partner's feet.

Finish the activity by reading Philippians 2:5–7 and if there's time, discuss with the group other practical ways of showing Jesus' love by serving each other. You could also sing 'The Servant King' together (*Mission Praise* 361).

Boy meets girl / girl meets boy

Imagine your ideal relationship with a member of the opposite sex … the boyfriend or girlfriend of your dreams! What qualities do you think you would look for? Now look at the list of qualities below and see if you can number them in order of importance. (There are no right answers and it will be difficult to do!) See if you can find all those qualities in the wordsearch – they're there somewhere!

affectionate	L	Y	H	T	R	O	W	T	S	U	R	T
caring	U	O	N	G	E	N	E	R	O	U	S	H
faithful												
fun	F	E	E	V	I	T	R	O	P	P	U	S
generous	H	C	O	R	I	N	L	O	Y	A	L	I
giving	T	N	T	H	I	A	O	N	H	S	K	F
honest												
kind	I	U	T	H	I	R	V	T	O	I	E	L
loving	A	F	F	E	C	T	I	O	N	A	T	E
loyal	F	E	N	V	S	F	N	D	E	O	U	S
supportive												
trustworthy	R	C	A	R	I	N	G	T	S	O	S	N
unselfish	G	N	I	V	I	G	E	V	T	E	N	U

Now write out the leftover letters, in order, in the spaces below:

— — — — — — — — — — — — — — — — — — — — — — — — — — — — — — — — — —

Find these verses in the Bible. When you have read them, see how many of the words from the wordsearch are mentioned, and tick them on the list when you've found them.

Do you think your boyfriend or girlfriend would be all of these things? **YES / NO**

Are you? **YES / NO**

Underline two things from the list you don't do very well, or aren't very good at. This week, why not try to work on them? You can't do it on your own, but God will help you if you ask him to. You could use this prayer, filling in the gaps:

Father God, I know that I'm not very good at ....

and .... This week, please help me to be more

.... and ....

Amen

14. Money

Introduction

Although this age group aren't normally super-rich, it's important for them to learn a Christian attitude to money at this stage, when all around them materialism is all-important. The activities focus on what the Bible says about wealth and our attitude towards possessions. There's an auction, a graffiti wall for the group to add to and activities to help the group think about the use and abuse of wealth.

Icebreaker (10 minutes)

Hold up a £50 note and ask the group to say or write down how they would spend it. Alternatively, you could give each group member a sealed envelope containing a cheque for £50 (or £100 or whatever figure you care to name!), made payable to them, and ask them to tell you what they would do with it!

Write the responses on a large sheet of paper or an OHP acetate and draw some conclusions about the results if appropriate.

Discussion questions (10 minutes)

1. What sort of things would a person living in the Third World buy with £50 – would they differ to this list? (Refer back to the icebreaker.)
2. 'Everything costs money somewhere along the line' True or false?
3. The Bible says, '… the love of money is a source of all kinds of evil' (1 Timothy 6:10). (This verse is often misquoted as, 'Money is the source of all kinds of evil,' whereas it's the love of it.)
   What does this mean? *Why* is the love of money a source of all kinds of evil?

Activity (15 minutes)

You will need: paper, lots of newspapers (including some copies of the *Financial Times*) scissors, glue, felt pens or crayons, Bibles.

As a group prepare two posters, one presented as a montage of newspaper cuttings referring to money, riches, wealth etc; the other showing what the Bible says about money with relevant verses (see following activities) copied out and illustrated if appropriate.

Activity (12 minutes)

Ask: 'Is wealth good or bad?' Photocopy this chart onto an OHP acetate (or copy it onto a large sheet of paper) and invite the group members to suggest good uses (eg providing security for home and family, helping others and sharing goods and money) and bad uses (eg wasting money, spending it on things like drugs, selfishly hoarding possessions etc). It may be a good idea to let the group members write up their own ideas if they want to, so that it is *their* chart, and they are actively involved in the discussion. When the lists are complete, show the Bible verses at the bottom of the chart.

Wealth	
Bad uses	Good uses
I want! I keep!	I share!
Making wealth your God leads to: Corruption (1 Timothy 6:9–10) Godlessness (Matthew 6:24) Stupidity (Luke 12:15)	Using wealth God's way leads to: Generosity (Luke 12:33–34) Practical help (1 Timothy 6:17–18) Encouragement (Acts 20:35)

Activity (20 minutes)

You will need: pencils and copies of the list for auction.

Set up an auction up as a TV-style game show. Have a dummy microphone and give the game a suitable name, such as 'Have a Bash with Cash' or 'Loadsa Lots'! Get the group to cheer and applaud to add to the fun and build up the atmosphere. Use a hammer for the auction and say 'Going, going, gone!' It's more realistic!

Rules

Each group member has £3000 (or whatever figure you choose) to spend, in multiples of £100. They select three 'lots' and decide how much they would be willing to spend on each, if necessary. (This figure goes in the first column). They bid for their choices, but if the lot is sold to a higher bidder, they can transfer the money allocated to it to another lot. If the price goes out of their range, and they don't get the item, then the selling price could be noted in the 'Top bid' column. If they do buy the item then the price they actually paid can go in the middle column. The auction is over when everything is sold or the money runs out!

	Lot no.	Amount I set aside	My highest bid	Top bid
1	International fame and popularity	....	....	....
2	A month's holiday anywhere in the world	....	....	....
3	A lovely mansion with a swimming pool	....	....	....
4	A long life free of illness	....	....	....
5	A new sports car	....	....	....
6	A world without violence or hatred	....	....	....
7	Lifetime financial security	....	....	....
8	As many clothes as I want	....	....	....
9	A chance to eliminate poverty	....	....	....
10	A complete library for my private use	....	....	....
11	A complete sound system	....	....	....
12	The love and admiration of friends	....	....	....
13	A world without prejudice	....	....	....
14	A happy family relationship	....	....	....

Debriefing

Once the auction has been completed, ask group members to underline the lots that they feel have Christian values. Then ask them to tick the lots which money *won't* buy. What could we do, if anything, to obtain those things? Are they all things that would benefit other people, or are some selfish? Is it OK to want them? Ask the group to share in pairs or with the whole group, why they chose their particular lots, and if there are any they would change now the auction is over.

Activity (15 minutes)

Use the 'What really matters?' sheet (individually or in groups) to examine a Bible story.

Activity (12 minutes)

Ask each group member to work out their own weekly or monthly income and expenditure and, if they have no objection, to share the results with the rest of the group! Are they happy with their personal budgets and the way they use their money? Has anything that the group has discussed influenced their attitude? If so, will they be making any changes to their spending habits? (Maybe the group leader should be prepared to contribute to this session!) The Bible stresses the importance of responsible regular and pro-portional giving (Deuteronomy 14:22). Is there any way in which the group members could give? (If not money, what about time, skills or food? Perhaps the group members could take responsibility for local needs, as well as obvious ones abroad.)

Game (8 minutes)

Photocopy, then cut out, these Bible verses and their references and pin at least one *verse* on each person's back. Mix up the *references* and distribute them as well (but in a different order!). Make sure each group member has a Good News Bible and get them to look up their reference, discover who's wearing it and collect it from that person. At the end of the game, find out some of what the Bible has to say about money by reading out the verses.

Keep your lives free from the love of money, and be satisfied with what you have.
Hebrews 13:5
Even if your riches increase, don't depend on them.
Psalm 62:10
Watch out and guard yourselves from every kind of greed …
Luke 12:15a
… a person's life is not made up of the things he owns, no matter how rich he may be.
Luke 12:15b
You cannot serve both God and money.
Luke 16:13
It will be very hard for rich people to enter the Kingdom of heaven.
Matthew 19:23
If you love money, you will never be satisfied.
Ecclesiastes 5:10
Those who want to get rich … are caught in the trap of many foolish and harmful desires.
1 Timothy 6:9
The love of money is a source of all kinds of evil.
1 Timothy 6:10
Stupid people spend their money as fast as they get it.
Proverbs 21:20
Why spend money on what does not satisfy? … Listen to me and do what I say, and you will enjoy the best food of all.
Isaiah 55:2
The law that you gave means more to me than all the money in the world.
Psalm 119:72

Songs

From heaven you came, helpless babe (*Mission Praise* 361)
Make me a channel of your peace (*Mission Praise* 153)
O give thanks to the Lord (*Mission Praise* 182)
Take my life and let it be (*Mission Praise* 212)
Peter and John went to pray ('silver and gold have I none')
    (*Mission Praise* 199)

Outside activity

Read Matthew 25:14–28 and then discuss how the group members could operate on the same principle. Using a float, give each member, say, £2 and ask them to find a way of doubling it by the following meeting. Suggest ways this could be done (eg by buying a bucket and sponge and then earning some money car washing or window cleaning, or maybe buying the ingredients to do some baking and then selling the results at school). The group may well come up with their own ideas! The money raised once the float has been deducted could be donated to a missionary society of the group's choice. (Another way of collecting for a missionary society is to save coppers in a glass jar or Smartie tube – it's surprising how quickly the total mounts!)

What really matters?

Read about a rich man in Mark 10:17–31 then circle the letter of the answer you think is right. The Bible verses will help you, so check back to them!

1. Why do you think the young man went to Jesus?

a He was trying to trick Jesus

b He wanted to live forever

c He wanted Jesus to see what a good person he was

d He wanted to become a follower of Jesus

e He liked to keep up to date with the latest religious ideas

f other ...

2. How did the young man feel about his life so far?

a Proud

b Ashamed

c Content

d In need of change

e Guilty

f Other ...

3. Why did Jesus ask him to give his money away?

a All rich people have to give up their money to follow Jesus

b To see what really mattered to him

c God can only use poor people

d To see if he would obey Jesus

e Jesus needed some ready cash

f Other ...

4. Why do you think the young man went away sad?

a He didn't want to give up his money

b He wished he had more to give up

c Other ...

Jesus' followers are called Christians. Does following Jesus have to be the most important thing in their lives?

And does this mean they have to give away everything they own?

In which Pooh is puzzled and Rabbit makes a discovery

Spring had come to the Forest. Pooh was walking happily in the sunshine, humming an occasional hum. He came to Rabbit's house. He could hear Rabbit hurrying about inside.

'Hallo, Rabbit,' called Pooh. 'Can I come in?'

The hurrying stopped.

'No!' said Rabbit shortly, and the hurrying started again.

'Well,' he said, 'shall I wait here for you to come out?'

'No,' said Rabbit again. 'I'm busy. Go away.'

Pooh scratched his nose. Rabbit was often busy. He felt important and enjoyed Organizing things, but he was not usually bad tempered. Something was wrong and it spoilt the morning.

'Bother!' said Pooh.

Next moment there was a small explosion, and Rabbit shot out of his house, straight past Pooh, and away in bounds through the heather.

Pooh was upset, Rabbit was different, and that made it a bothering sort of day. So he went to find his friend Piglet.

Piglet was sitting in the sun outside his house, trying to decide whether he preferred yellow crocuses to purple ones. He had just given up and was being glad that he had both, when Pooh stumped along.

'Hallo, Piglet,' said Pooh, 'Can I come in?'

'No,' said Piglet, 'You can go in if you like, but you can't *come* in because I'm out.'

'Oh,' said Pooh, slowly. 'Well, can I stay out with you, Piglet, because I want to talk to you?'

'Yes,' said Piglet, 'and I'll bring a little smackerel of something for the two of us.'

About half an hour later, Pooh wiped his mouth with the back of his furry paw.

'Piglet,' he said, 'I'm worried about Rabbit. He's different.'

'Yes,' said Piglet sadly. 'It's because one of his rich friends-and-relations has left him some money. Like the rest of us he never had any before. Now he keeps counting it and hiding it and investing it …'

'But Rabbit doesn't wear a vest,' said Pooh.

'Pooh,' said Piglet severely, 'it isn't like that.'

'I'm sorry,' said Pooh humbly, 'I thought it wouldn't be.'

'The trouble is,' went on Piglet. 'that he used to be kind to Kanga and Baby Roo and you and me, and he always remembered his friends-and-relations' birthdays. And now all he thinks about is his money. What can we do?'

'I know! ' shouted Pooh so suddenly that Piglet fell off the log on which he had been sitting and had to be dusted.

'I'll go and see what the others think. It's always better with All of Us.'

'Pooh, said Piglet admiringly, 'that's a very good plan. And I haven't anything to do until after lunch tomorrow so I'll come with you.'

They chatted of this and that as they walked through the Forest, until they came to the Gloomy Place where Eeyore was.

'Hallo, Eeyore,' said Pooh.

'Good morning, Pooh. Good morning, little Piglet,' said Eeyore, 'which it's not,' said he, 'but I suppose we might as well pretend.'

'Why, what's the matter, Eeyore?' said Piglet anxiously.

'A thunderstorm,' said Eeyore.

Pooh and Piglet both glanced nervously at the pale blue sky.

'Here,' said Eeyore heavily, 'just now. It came just before you did, and it *crashed* into me. I've no breath left.' He sighed deeply.

'Oh, Eeyore!' said Piglet.

'Rabbit,' he said impressively. 'It was Rabbit.'

'What did he say, Eeyore?' asked Pooh, impatiently.

'Nothing,' said Eeyore. 'He went.'

'What can we *do*, Eeyore?'

'Nothing,' said Eeyore gloomily. 'He won't listen. He can't even see us, not so as to get out of the way. He's set in his own way and that's the end of it. It'll be the end of *him* too, I shouldn't wonder. Money!' he said. 'Ha!'

Pooh and Piglet were trying to think of something hopeful to say, when a shadow fell across the grass and Owl was with them.

'Oh, Owl!' said Pooh, before Owl could begin to talk, 'You are very clever, Owl.'

Owl blinked appreciatively and was about to tell Pooh what a very perceptive bear he was, when Pooh said quickly,

'What's the matter with Rabbit and how can we cure him, Owl?' Owl settled himself comfortably on a low branch.

'Our friend Rabbit,' said Owl, 'has inherited a legacy.'

'What the matter with his legs?' asked Piglet, really wanting to know. 'I said "legacy",' said Owl severely, 'a pecuniary emolument.' 'Oh,' said Piglet meekly. Pooh opened his mouth and then closed it again.

'This legacy or inheritance,' went on Owl, warming to his subject, 'has assumed in his eyes the proportion of an all embracing interest. As a result, his attitude has become incompatible with that of his creator. Corruption has severed him from the very root of his existence …'

Owl's voice continued to rise and fall, and as the sun was getting hotter they closed their eyes and left it to each other to listen to what Owl was saying.

Pooh awoke with a start and said, 'Yes Owl, of course, Owl, just as you were saying, but we must be getting along, musn't we, Piglet?'

Piglet was dreaming that he lived in a giant crocus and couldn't find the door, so he was quite glad for Pooh to hurry him off. They left Owl, still talking to Eeyore who was still asleep.

'We must go and see Kanga,' said Pooh earnestly. 'She's very sensible and will know just what to do.'

Kanga was busy spring-cleaning and trying to stop Baby Roo from spring-dirtying everything when she'd cleaned it, so they were both glad to see Piglet and Pooh.

Roo listened with mounting excitement and began to jump up and down and squeak delightedly, 'Rabbit's gone potty, that's what it is. Rabbit's …'

'Hush, Roo, dear,' said Kanga severely. 'Someone might hear you! Now go and play over there,' she said more kindly 'where we can all see you.' She lowered her voice, so that Roo, who had stopped squeaking and jumping and was listening hard, could scarcely hear.

'The trouble with Rabbit,' she said, 'is that he has become greedy. Because he has some money, he wants more and more. He thinks money is the only thing worth having, and can't see that there are much more important things in life. Now why are we standing here talking when there's so much work to do? Come along. We'll all help.'

Piglet suddenly remembered that what he had decided to do tomorrow afternoon had been tomorrow afternoon yesterday, which meant that it had to be done today, so he hurried off, trying to remember what it was.

Pooh murmured politely, 'No thank you, Kanga,' to the brush that she offered him, and went off to the top of the Forest.

Christopher Robin was just coming out of his house when Pooh appeared.

'Hallo, silly old bear!' he said affectionately. 'Where shall we go?'

'Anywhere,' said Pooh happily.

So they did.

And as they went they talked, and as they talked Pooh thought, and for a bear of Very Little Brain it was a very thinking sort of thought.

'Christopher Robin.'

'Yes, Pooh.'

'Do you have money?'

'A little pocket money.'

'And it hasn't made you, well, … like Rabbit?'

'I don't think so,' said Christopher Robin slowly. 'They give it to you, so it's nothing to be proud of. And I don't keep it; I spend it to buy something nice and useful. After all, extract of malt is better for Tiggers to eat than money.'

Pooh looked hopeful.

'And there's honey,' said Christopher.

'That's just what I think,' said Pooh. 'There is. But what can we do for Rabbit?'

'I'll talk to him,' said Christopher Robin carelessly.

Some weeks later, when the Spring couldn't decide whether it was Summer or not, Pooh was walking through the heather and found himself near Rabbit's house. Rabbit came out, sniffed the air and saw Pooh.

'Hallo,' he said, 'just in time for a little something.'

'Really?' said Pooh doubtfully, as he followed Rabbit into his house. And there on the shelves, where his money boxes had been, were bundles of thistles, boxes of haycorns and jars of honey …

'But I thought you didn't like honey,' said Pooh half an hour later. 'No, but you do,' said Rabbit.

Videos

Rich Man, Poor Man This video deals very well with worldly attitudes towards riches and success. It asks the question, 'What is the most valuable thing of all?' An excellent discussion starter. (15 minutes – CRP/Scripture Union)

McGee and Me – Do the Bright Thing Nicholas learns about how decisions are made. (30 minutes – CRP)

'Enry 'Enry normally loafs about watching television, until he wins the pools! An imaginative re-telling of the parable of the rich fool. (15 minutes CRP/Scripture Union)

Graffiti wall

(To be copied onto a large sheet of paper for group members to add to and scribble on as they wish)

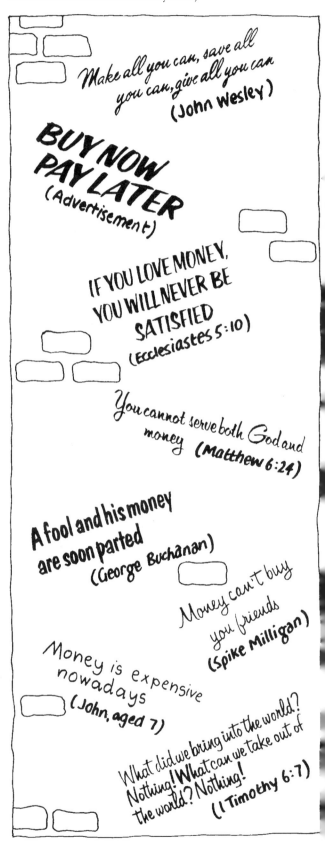

Introduction

A mock election, a quick game of 'Just a minute', discussion questions and a quiz – all are ways to get this age group thinking about an issue which in some ways will be very remote. After all, it will be a few years yet before they can vote! However, it's not too soon to encourage them to take an interest in the way their country is governed, and to examine policies and decisions from a Christian point of view. With so many social problems demanding attention in today's society, an awareness of the needs now will help shape Christian attitudes for the voters of the future.

Icebreaker (8 minutes)

Ask the group to sit in a circle. The first person says, 'If I were prime minister I would …' and suggests one thing he or she would do. The second person repeats what the first person has said and then adds his or her own statement. This continues around the circle. Anyone who misses out any of the statements is out.

Icebreaker (10 minutes)

Play 'Just a minute' with the group. You will need to chair the show and appoint a scorekeeper and a timekeeper (who will need a watch with a second hand). In turn, the other group members are given a minute to speak on the subject of 'Our government'. They are not allowed to hesitate, or repeat a key word during their minute. If they do, anyone else in the group may challenge them by standing up. The chairman has to decide if the challenge of 'hesitation' or 'repetition' is a fair one. If so, the challenger continues on the same subject for the remainder of the time, with two bonus points for a correct challenge. If not, the original speaker continues and the challenger loses two bonus points for an incorrect challenge. When the minute is up, the whistle should be blown. Whoever is speaking when the whistle is blown is awarded five points. The winner is the one with the most points.

Outside activities

Arrange a visit to your local council to see a debate and/or for a guided tour. This can be arranged by contacting your local councillor. (The council offices can give you his or her address or phone number.) Or plan a visit to the Houses of Parliament. This could be arranged through your local MP. You can contact them by writing to the House of Commons, Westminster, London.

Game (10 minutes)

You will need: newspaper pictures (see below) and paper and pencils for each group member.

Cut out pictures of politicians (local, national and international) from newspapers and magazines. Number them and display them round the room. Individuals or teams have to identify them. They score one point for getting the right name and another for saying what the politician's job is, eg foreign secretary, mayor of Puddletown, president of the USA.

Quiz (15 minutes)

This quiz shows that there are a lot of politicians in the Bible! The group members will need good Bible knowledge to be able to participate, but there are quite a few clues to help them, especially if the first letter of the answer is given at the beginning of each question. Divide the group into two teams and ask the questions alternately, reading out the clues one at a time, to give the team three chances to identify the politician. You will need to appoint a scorekeeper who will give three points if the politician is identified from the first clue, two from the second clue, and one from the third.

1. 'J' – Sold for twenty pieces of silver; falsely accused of rape; prime minister of Egypt. (Joseph)
2. 'N' – An exile in Babylon; cup-bearer to a king; rebuilder of walls. (Nehemiah)
3. 'D' – A vegetarian; an interpreter of dreams; adviser to the king of Babylon. (Daniel)
4. 'J' – His foreign policy advice was ignored; thrown down a well; wrote Lamentations. (Jeremiah)
5. 'P' – His wife had strange dreams; he washed his hands at Jesus' trial; Roman governor. (Pilate)
6. 'M' – Sat at the gate of Susa in sackcloth; overheard the wicked Haman's plot; became adviser to the king. (Mordecai)
7. 'D' – Prophetess; ruled Israel for over forty years; defeated an enemy army. (Deborah)
8. 'Q of S' – Ruler of a distant country; wanted wisdom; came to visit King Solomon. (Queen of Sheba)
9. 'M' – Chief negotiator with Pharaoh on behalf of the Israelites; unsuccessful at first; able to plague the life of the king of Egypt. (Moses)
10. 'S' – As a young boy, lived in the temple with Eli; God spoke to him in a dream; anointed David as King of Israel. (Samuel)

Bible focus (30 minutes x 2 sessions)

Outline the story of Esther. You could use the Superbook cartoon video (see suggestions for videos). It's a story of political intrigue involving issues that are still important today, eg the role of women and the place of ethnic minorities.

Divide the group up into twos or threes, and give each small group a section of the story of Esther to work on. Their brief is to produce a TV script for a Persian television company, relating to their part of the story; eg chapter 2 – the Miss Persian Empire Beauty Contest, chapter 3 – background report on the Jews in Persia, chapter 6 – a crime report on a plot against the king, chapters 7 and 8 – a news story on the death of Haman, chapters 8 and 9 – an interview with Mordecai or Esther. Come back together to read or perform the scripts in sequence.

Discuss with the group where God was in the story. He didn't get a mention by name but he was actively involved through people who trusted him and were willing to serve him whatever the cost. So where is God in modern-day politics? He's not often mentioned by name but he's actively involved through people who trust him and are willing to serve him whatever the cost. There are people like that in all the main political parties.

Activity (15 minutes)

You will need: the 'Christians and politics' chart, photocopied or copied onto an overhead projector acetate (or enlarged on a sheet of paper), pens and Bibles for each small group.

Divide the group into six small groups and give each group a Bible reference to find (see list below). Ask them to be ready to read them out to the rest of the group at the appropriate moment. Display the chart, with the six statements covered up with strips of paper.

Go through the chart in order, and as each statement is reached uncover it and ask the relevant group to read out the Bible verse(s). Ask everyone to decide what word is missing and get a group member to fill it in. Add a few comments (see below) before moving on to the next statement.

1. Romans 13:1 ('authority' – if possible, read this verse from the Living Bible, as it is a helpful paraphrase.)
2. 1 Peter 2:13–15 ('obey' – Christians should be peaceful, considerate, and law-abiding.)
3. 1 Timothy 2:1–2 ('pray' – those governing our country need our prayers, so that they exercise their God-given authority wisely.)
4. Acts 4:18–20 ('disobey' – under certain circumstances, such as in this story, Christians cannot obey the law if it conflicts with biblical principles.)
5. Ephesians 6:5–9 ('workers' – again, the Living Bible paraphrases these verses in a helpful way. Refer to Joseph's story in Genesis 39:1–5.)
6. Luke 12:7 ('people' – Christians should put people before things. A political movement that doesn't value people is wrong.)

Activity (10 minutes)

Ask the group if they feel there would be a place in our political system for a 'Christian Party'. Suggest that for, say, five minutes, they give some thought to specific Christian policies for the following: Health; Education; Environment; Employment; Economy; Defence. Allocate one subject per small group.

When the time is up, quickly get each group to report back, outlining their policies. Briefly discuss the results. Suggest that the group write to CARE Trust* for further information, and when it arrives, use it to help them pray for the government, and Christians involved in politics.

*CARE Trust, 53 Romney Street, London SW1F 3RF. (They publish a regular news magazine and supply a wide range of materials on political issues relating to the Christian faith.)

Activity (20 minutes)

You will need: a copy of the manifestos (see opposite) for the candidates, enough pencils and ballot papers for each group member and a ballot box. You will also need to select three group members to be candidates, and two others to be scrutineers. (This could be done in advance.) If possible, set up a 'voting booth' to add to the sense of occasion – an up-ended table would do! You could act as returning officer.

Explain to the group that they are going to hold a mock election! Three candidates have been nominated: Mr/Ms Brown, Mr/Ms Pink and Mr/Ms White. They will each present their manifesto, and after the group members have cast their vote, the one receiving the largest number of votes will be elected as Member of Parliament for the local constituency.

Ask the three candidates to present their manifestos in turn. Issue the ballot papers and get the scrutineers to organise a queue for voting! When all the votes have been cast, and counted, you could announce the results ceremonially as follows:

'I (your name), being the returning officer for the electoral district of (name of the local area), hereby declare the results of the election as follows: Mr/Ms Brown … votes, Mr/Ms Pink … votes, Mr/Ms White … votes. I therefore declare (name of winner) to be the elected Member of Parliament for this constituency.'

Ask the group members to say why they voted the way they did. Which policies did they think were good? Which were bad? Which candidate advocated Christian policies?

Mr/Ms Brown's manifesto

I recognise the serious problems in Northern Ireland and advocate a scheme of power-sharing between Catholics and Protestants.

I believe more money should be spent on housing.

Further education must be expanded. Christian education in schools should be maintained rather than abandoned. Nursery education should be developed naturally. Too many young people who want to earn their living are compelled against their will to remain at school. The school leaving age should therefore be lowered to 15 while encouraging those who wish to remain at school to do so.

Industry should be encouraged to export more to maintain our balance of payments.

Local decision-making in politics should be encouraged.

Mr/Ms Pink's manifesto

Old age pensions should be increased. Many decent old people are suffering through inflation and must be given additional financial support.

Too little is being done about housing. My scheme would produce an extra 200,000 houses a year. This would reduce the waiting list for council homes and enable young married couples to purchase homes of their own.

Inflation is at the root of our problems. As money loses its value society grows more unstable. Government controls must be imposed rigidly to restore our stability.

I am in favour of community activities. Sports centres and recreational activities should exist in every town to help our young people. I would provide money from public funds to achieve this.

Our educational system is being ruined by constant examinations. They do more harm than good. Exams should be abolished.

Mr/Ms White's manifesto

I believe in getting things done. My aim will be to make this country great again by getting rid of all foreigners. Immigrants must go! Englishmen are losing their jobs because we have opened our country to people who shouldn't be here. Those immigrants who haven't pinched our jobs are pinching our dole money! A lot of these foreigners have just come to England to live off the State. They get free social benefits, free medical treatment and they don't have to lift a finger to work. I repeat, immigrants must go!

Great Britain must regain her Empire. We must go out to conquer distant lands and civilise them. We must expand our borders and use our splendid Army to gain territories rich in mineral wealth.

We must not be afraid to use violence. Violence is noble and heroic. Those who stand in our way must be crushed underfoot. Our factories must produce more weapons. This will have two advantages. First, more jobs will be created, thus reducing unemployment. Second, our armed forces will be strengthened, other nations will learn to fear us and we shall be a great nation again.

Ballot paper	
Brown	
Pink	
White	

Christians and politics
a guide to Christian action

God gives ....
to governments to rule.
(Romans 13:1)

Christians should .... the law.
(1 Peter 2:13–15)

Christians should ....
for rulers and governments.
(1 Timothy 2:1–2)

Christians may sometimes have to

.... the law.
(Acts 4:18–20)

Christians should be good ....
(Ephesians 6:5–9)

Christians should put ....
before things.
(Luke 12:7)

Prayer ideas

- Get a large map of the world. Cut out photos of world leaders from newspapers and stick them on the appropriate places on the map. Use the map as a prayer guide. The book *Operation World* (published by STL) will provide a huge amount of useful information on every country in the world.
- Get the group members to write to your local mp and councillors asking them specifically what they would like the group to pray for, then pray about it!
- Use the 'Prayabout' sheets, either by photocopying them for each group member to use individually or by reading some extracts as part of a time of corporate prayer.

Songs

Lord for the years (*Mission Praise* 142)
Restore, O Lord, the honour of thy name (*Mission Praise* 196)

Worship

Find out when and where your local Civic Service takes place (often after the choosing of the new mayor). Why not go to it as a group?

Book suggestion

Piggy in the Middle (by Christine Harris, published by Scripture Union) is the story of a girl caught up in her mother's campaign to save the local hospital. You could serialise this for the group.

Videos

Under the Shadow – The Dividing Wall This powerful documentary, intended as a discussion starter, brings together an ex-IRA hunger-striker and a member of the Ulster Volunteer Force. They relate their experiences of being on opposite sides of the religious and political wall dividing Northern Ireland. (This is recommended for the 14+ age-range, so your group may be too young to appreciate it.) (22 minutes – CRP/Scripture Union)

Superbook 1, Vol 8 – Esther A cartoon series, featuring the story of Esther. (30 minutes – CRP)

Animal Farm This cartoon version of George Orwell's famous novel does not have any Christian content, but is a powerful parable about corruption in political leaders and the use and abuse of power. (70 minutes – CRP)

Prayabout:
The government

Underline any of these statements (all from readers of **One to One** Bible notes) that help you say to God what you want to about the government. Then use them to start your own prayers about it.

Lord, here's what the government does …

- It runs the country and handles our relationships with other countries
- It looks after places
- It tries to help people who haven't much money or a home to live in
- It decides what is right for the country and tries to find answers to all the problems
- It makes policies to collect taxes and pay for education
- It gives grants so that, if you want to build on to your house, you can
- It helps to make living easier
- It provides money for charities and buys weapons
- It tries to make the country how they want it
- It puts up the price of things
- It makes up laws
- It tries to keep law and order, and find jobs for unemployed people
- It is a group of people who are elected to represent everyone and introduce changes to everyday life
- It is made up of politicians who shout at each other

Lord I think the best thing about being prime minister would be …

- Telling people off and telling them if their ideas are right or wrong
- Being a kind of figurehead
- Having the street closed off so that nobody could get to my house
- Everybody would do as I say
- Being on TV
- Putting up the price of cigarettes so that everyone stops smoking
- Getting the world how I want it
- Going to foreign places to look at wild life and meet other prime ministers
- Having enough money for a big, furnished house with five telephones
- Helping poor people here and in other countries
- Seeing that the people like me
- Sending out food to famine areas
- Telling everyone off for dropping litter
- Being able to afford a new bike

The hardest thing would be …

- All the work!
- Having to face continual criticism because of different ideas about how the country should be run
- Having to pose for photos all the time
- Deciding whether to scrap nuclear weapons or not
- Having the confidence in myself to make decisions
- Knowing people may try to kill me
- Not letting anyone down
- Getting people to like what I want to do
- Trying to keep the world nice and tidy
- Knowing what to do
- Having to close down a factory, so people lose their jobs

Lord, I'd really like the government to …

- Stop all firearms, guns and explosives getting into the country and make them illegal
- Make it so that people don't have to live in slums with little children
- Stop wars, violence, drugs and other crimes
- Outlaw CFCs
- Prevent life being destroyed
- Do something about racism
- Give more money to the poor
- Give everyone a home and a job
- Get rid of **all** bombs
- Make all petrol unleaded
- Stop people dropping litter
- Make all world leaders friends
- Do something to help our environment and all the wild animals
- Stop pollution and using animals for tests in laboratories
- Stick to their word about environmental issues
- Do what **you** want rather than what **they** want

Introduction

In this material, the group members will be able to find out about various types of prejudice and then think about the ways in which they personally react to prejudice. They can then see what the Bible says about prejudice and what a Christian response should be towards people from other backgrounds, countries, age-groups etc. There are some telling puzzles which will expose unacknowledged prejudices as well as a couple of sketchscripts, 'Bible focus' material and a look at the story of the Ugly Duckling!

Icebreaker (10 minutes)

You will need: paper and pens for everyone or photocopies of the chart shown below.

Either copy the chart and display it to the group, or give out the photocopies.

Ask group members to write the names of some famous people in the spaces at the top and then to give each person marks out of ten in each category. (This could be done corporately, or individually if you use photocopies.)

name:	....	....	....
	....	....	....
	Score	Score	Score
wealth	....	....	....
age	....	....	....
clothes	....	....	....
looks	....	....	....
hairstyle	....	....	....
physical strength	....	....	....

Ask the group if they think it is a good way of judging people.

Read the story of David being anointed King of Israel – 1 Samuel 16:1–13 (you may find it helpful to put the story in context first). It could be done as a dramatised reading, with a narrator, Samuel, the LORD, city leaders and Jesse. The last part of verse 7 – ' Man looks at the outward appearance but I look at the heart' (said the LORD) would be a good point to draw out of the reading and it would be an excellent verse to encourage the group to memorise!

Finish this activity by reading James 2:1–4, 8–9.

Icebreaker (8 minutes)

You will need: a washable felt pen (preferably dark brown!)

The aim is to get the group united talking to each other, and mixing amongst themselves, *without prejudice.* (Point this out when the game is over!)

As they arrive at the meeting each person receives a number of 'felt-tip freckles' (to a maximum of six) just behind their left ear. When most people have arrived do some getting together exercises as follows.

1. Everyone must find out how many freckles they have and locate everyone in the room who has the same number. When found they should sit as a group on the floor.
2. Now they know their own number, do some quick puzzles with them, such as look for the first group to sit down with a total of eighteen freckles, etc!

Activity (10 minutes)

You will need: a set of pictures (cut from magazines) to portray up to ten different sorts of people, such as sportspeople, students, businesspeople, etc.

The aim is to show that it is very easy to judge people on first sight by what we see, or by what we think we know.

Have the pictures displayed around the walls and ask the group members to go around the room and make mental notes on the answers to question such as:
- What job does this person have?
- How intelligent are they?
- Is he/she a Christian?
- Are they married?

When you've completed the task sit down in groups of four, try and place the characters in order of importance. What makes a person most important or least important? How do we judge people? Read Matthew 7:1–6 together, to finish this activity.

Puzzle (3 minutes)

The blind beggar

Here's a puzzle which is so simple that it baffles even the most intelligent. Some of you will get the answer immediately, others will have heard it before. If you think you know the answer, please don't shout it out: just put up a hand, and when everyone's had a chance to think about it, I'll ask someone to give us the answer. Okay, here it is.

'The blind beggar had a brother who died. But the man who died didn't have any brothers. What was the relationship between the blind beggar and the man who died?'

It's worth repeating the question two or three times, giving people a bit of time to think about it. As hands go up point out that most people think that there must be some religious answer to it like 'they were monks'. Assure your audience that if they're thinking along these lines they're way off. Some hands will go down. If there are adults present remind them that they too can join in.

Once you're sure that everyone has understood the question and had plenty of time to think about it, ask for answers, trying to make sure that you avoid those who have heard it before. The correct answer is, of course, sister and brother, for the blind beggar was a woman.

All becomes clear – how is it that so many of us don't see something so simple? The reason is that we are blinded by a preconception, namely that all blind beggars must be male. Why do we think that? There must be about as many female blind beggars as there are male ones. Is it perhaps to do with our biblical background? It's hard to say. One thing is certain, that preconceptions can block out simple answers. If we could somehow get rid of our false conceptions and prejudices we might find other simple answers to baffling questions.

What is most alarming is that many of our strongest prejudices are formed at a very early age.

In its worst form, prejudice can make us blind to the needs of others – even people close to us: perhaps we're all just a bunch of blind beggars, whose brothers and sisters are slipping away before our sightless eyes.

Game (10 minutes)

You will need: a set of instruction cards which should encourage discrimination against people wearing certain colours. Possible instructions are:
- stick your tongue out at someone wearing red
- ignore anyone wearing blue
- shout at someone wearing purple
- blow a raspberry at someone wearing green.

Have sufficient cards for at least one each (you can double up on some instructions). Hand out a card to each group member then allow five minutes for them to discover as many of the other rules of discrimination as possible, *whilst still following the rule on their own card*.

Follow-up discussion

Start a discussion with these questions.

- We don't normally act in such an irrational way towards colour.
- Why then do some people react negatively towards people with different colour skin?
- Ask the group if they can name any other areas of irrational prejudice (race, class, accent, age, sex, wealth, intelligence, occupation etc).

Videos

The Dark Side of the Gate A science-fiction adventure set in a future society where winning is everything and losers are despised. Useful for promoting discussion on prejudice. (18 minutes – Scripture Union/CRP)

The Ballad of Vincent and Kevin This very funny and telling poem is a modern-day version of the parable of the Good Samaritan. Vincent is a black teenager from Yorkshire who gets beaten up on a day-trip to London. His rescuer is someone who at first sight seems most unlikely … (6 minutes – Scripture Union/CRP)

Bible focus (12 minutes)

You will need: a set of 'Match the passage' cards (photocopied in advance), *Blu-tack* to stick them on the wall, Bibles, paper and pens (enough for each group member)

'Match the passage' cards

… I solemnly call upon you to obey these instructions without showing any prejudice or favour to anyone in anything you do.
1 Timothy 5:21
Have the same concern for everyone. Do not be proud, but accept humble duties.
Romans 12:16
Don't plan anything that will hurt your neighbour; he lives beside you, trusting you.
Proverbs 3:29
If you laugh at poor people, you insult the God who made them. You will be punished if you take pleasure in someone's misfortune.
Proverbs 17:5
Remember what I told you: 'No slave is greater than his master.' If they persecuted me they will persecute you too.
John 15:20

Place the cards around the outside of the room and explain the rules to the group.

Game 1 Using a Bible to help, try to match the text with the reference. Note it down on a piece of paper, it might be useful in the second half of the game.

Game 2 Leader reads out either a text or a reference. Group have to run to and stand beside that text or reference's partner. Last person there gets a penalty point. (Players are out after three penalty points.)

Sketchscript (5 minutes)

Cast: Harold, Wendy; narrator.
Props: newspaper; book; knitting; two chairs; baby doll in a shawl.

Harold shakes out and re-folds his newspaper; the noise of it seems to annoy his wife, Wendy, who puts aside her library book and reaches for her knitting needles as if to fight back. He reads for a moment, then folds the paper in quarters and chucks it onto the floor.

HAROLD: Honestly, Christmas Eve and the blooming TV has to go on the blink. Typical!

WENDY: Yes, and ten to one when we call the man out on the 27th it'll behave perfectly as soon as he gets here …

HAROLD: And go wonky again just in time for the New Year … What was that?

WENDY: What was what?

HAROLD: Sounded like a knock at the door.

WENDY: I didn't hear anything.

HAROLD: I'm sure I heard something.

WENDY: Probably carol singers.

HAROLD: I don't hear any singing.

Pause

WENDY: Well, if you're so sure, go and have a look.

HAROLD: Alright, alright.

Exit

WENDY: Well?

HAROLD: No one there … hang on though, what's this?

WENDY: What's what?

HAROLD: Someone's left a package on our doorstep.

WENDY: Oh my God, Harold, don't touch it, it's probably a bomb!

HAROLD: *(Enters with bundle)*: It isn't a bomb, dear … It's a baby!

WENDY: *(Rising and letting out a little shriek)*: Well, what did you bring it in for?

HAROLD: What do you mean?

WENDY: You fool! Someone's probably left it there and waited to see if we'd take it in, and now that you have, we're responsible for it.

HAROLD: Who'd do a thing like that?

WENDY: Gypsies! Look how dark his skin is.

HAROLD: Shh, you'll wake him … And anyway, gypsies don't abandon their children and most of them don't have skin any darker than you or I.

WENDY: I don't care, we'll have to get rid of it. Phone the police.

HAROLD: *(Suddenly worried)*: Hang on a minute, not the police, shouldn't we phone the RSPCA or something?

WENDY: Not the RSPCA, you mean the NSPCC.

HAROLD: That's the one. You phone them, they'll be in the phone book. *(Exit Wendy)* Hey, I think he's waking up … Wow! Look at those eyes! Hello there, my little prince.

Enter Wendy

WENDY: There's no reply of course, I mean they're hardly likely to be manning the phones on Christmas Eve.

HAROLD: Look at him, dear – there you go, little fellow – look at him laughing … not crying, have you ever seen such a peaceful baby? I feel like I could sit and look into those eyes forever … Couldn't we keep him, just over-night, then we could find out who to contact in the morning … and maybe we could even keep him longer than that, you know, give him a home if he really doesn't have one …

WENDY: *(During this speech she has begun to play with the baby, now she suddenly catches herself)* No! No, I'm sorry, Harold, but it's out of the question … I'm sure he's very nice and all that but, but …

HAROLD: But what?

WENDY: But, well – he's not ours, and he's probably not even an English baby … I'm sorry but it's out of the question. I can't be doing with babies in the house, what with feeding and crying and nappies … I just can't be doing with it, Harold. I'll have a breakdown I swear I will …

HAROLD: Fine, fine, but what are we going to do with him?

WENDY: I don't know, but you'll have to think of something – you're the head of the house. After all, what would the neighbours say if we suddenly produced a baby without any warning … and *(They both look at each other)*

HAROLD and WENDY: The Neighbours!

WENDY: Quickly, Harold, before it starts crying.

HAROLD: Right, come along, little prince. You're going to meet the Robertsons. *(Exit with bundle)*

Wendy sits biting nails or paces up and down. Enter Harold, flops in chair.

WENDY: Well?

HAROLD: Perfect. I nipped over the wall, popped him on the doorstep, rang the bell and was back over the wall and out of sight by the time old man Robertson had answered it, and he definitely took it in! We're in the clear!

WENDY: Well done! What's that?

HAROLD: I'm not sure. I found it on our doorstep as I was coming back in, must have been under the carrycot. Oh it's alright, it's just one of those circulars from the parish church or something. *(He sits again and picks up the paper.)*

WENDY: What's it say?

HAROLD: Dunno. *(Glances at leaflet again.)* Something about the Prince of Peace. *(Resumes reading paper – she resumes knitting or reading.)*

(Enter Narrator)

NARRATOR: There is a legend that each Christmas Eve the Christ Child is laid on a doorstep in a different town. As he is passed from house to house and street to street he never cries: but often Christmas morning finds him still left outside, freezing and alone.

Bible focus (15 minutes)

You will need: Bibles, paper, pens and lists of texts to be used.

The aim of this activity is to discover well known characters who suffered prejudice and to look at Jesus' reaction to people who were normally victims of prejudice. Divide into small groups and give each group a list of Bible references.

> Set A: Matthew 12:9–14; Matthew 15:21–28
> Set B: Mark 6:1–6; Mark 10:13–16
> Set C: Luke 18:35–43; John 8:1–11

Ask the three groups to find their verses and then decide who suffered prejudice and why. After, say, four or five minutes, have a quick 'feedback' from each small group. Ask whether these sort of things still happen today.

Get the same small groups to look at Jesus' reaction to people who were normally prejudiced. Can they answer the following questions for each character?
- Why were some of the people that Jesus met prejudiced?
- Can you name some modern day prejudices of this type?
- How would you have reacted had you met the people involved? (Be as honest as you dare.)
- What was Jesus' reaction?

Story (20 minutes)

Read or listen to a tape of the familiar story of the Ugly Duckling. (There is a very good Ladybird version available.) The story speaks for itself, but briefly discuss the following points:
- Can you identify the different types of prejudice in the story?
- Why did everyone dislike the duckling so much? What does it tell us about them?
- Was it fair?
- Does anything like this story ever happen at your school, perhaps with someone who is new, or clumsy, or not very clever? If so, what could you do about it?

Discussion (10 minutes)

(The Bible verses are listed to aid discussion rather than give the right answers to the questions.)
- What should a Christian attitude to other people be?
  Matthew 5:43–48; James 2:1–9
- What can you do if you think that you have got into the habit of judging other people?
  Romans 12:2; 1 John 1:8–9
- Should Christians try to put on an act to try and attract non-Christians to Christ?
  Matthew 5:16; James 2:14–18
- What can your group do as a whole to be attractive and welcoming to visitors?
  Romans 15:1–6; 1 Corinthians 9:20–22

Prayer (15 minutes)

Start by getting the group members to focus on times when, for whatever reason, they have pre-judged others. Remind them that it's something that we all do, and that it's our attitude and the things we *think*, as much as the things we say and do, which are wrong. For them, it may be people at school that they have judged or discriminated against. Encourage them to tell God about this and to name any people that they have treated unfairly. Emphasise that God forgives us if we are really sorry and we ask him to. (Read 1 John 1:9 aloud to the group at this point.)

Now suggest that the group members form small groups of two and three and briefly identify groups of people who are victims of prejudice. (Eg disabled people, Jewish people, black people etc.) After a couple of minutes ask them to pray in their small groups for these people, either aloud in turn around the group, or quietly. (If they are shy about praying out loud, suggest they pass Bible around the group. Whoever is holding it prays, but if they don't want to pray aloud they can simply pass it straight on to the next person.)

Sketchscript: On the road to Camelot
(20 minutes)

This is an ambitious sketch – more like a mini-play. It will need a lot of rehearsing. You have been warned … but it will be worth the effort!

Cast: Three narrators; man; knights and maidens (any number!); Sir Lancelot; bishop; man from West Wales.

(Scene opens with a freeze of knights and maidens at a banquet. Knight and maiden with speaking parts 'unfreeze' while they say their lines, them 're-freeze' when Narrator One has finished speaking to them.)

NARRATOR ONE: Long ago, when King Arthur ruled in Camelot, when knights were bold and maidens were fair, …

MAIDEN: But I've got brown hair!

NARRATOR ONE: I don't mean fair – blonde, I mean fair – pretty.

MAIDEN: Well why didn't you say so?

NARRATOR ONE: Uhumm! Long, long ago, when King Arthur ruled in Camelot, when knights were bold and maidens were pretty, when dragons were fierce, …

KNIGHT: Dragons! Don't be silly, there's no such thing as dragons!

NARRATOR ONE: OK! It's not really that important. Do you mind letting me continue with the story so that we can get finished before it's my dinner time? Right! Long, long ago, when King Arthur ruled in Camelot, when knights were bold and maidens were pretty, when dragons, if there were any, were fierce … *(Pause to see if any more interruptions are likely, then continues when satisfied)* England was not just one country, but consisted of many smaller nations, constantly at war with each other.

(Knights and maidens now split into two halves one either side of the stage and become the warring nations of Wessex and West Wales.)

NARRATOR TWO: Those from Wessex and those from West Wales were particularly nasty to each other. There were duels … *(One from each side steps forward. They stand back to back, advance ten paces away from each other, turn and fire. Both are shot and are dragged off by fellow countrymen.)* and they certainly never sent each other Christmas cards. *(The two sides turn their backs on their opposing countrymen.)*

NARRATOR THREE: Nobody knew how or why the squabbling started, they just knew that they were not on speaking terms.

(Stage clears, all except for 'Man' from Wessex and his family. The following action takes place as each narrator tells it.)

NARRATOR TWO: One day, one of the citizens of Wessex set off on a long journey. He said good-bye to his wife and family and headed off on his horse. His horse was a good old nag, and very comfortable to ride. So after a while he dozed off to sleep. When he awoke he didn't know where he was at all!

NARRATOR ONE: Then suddenly, three evil robbers leapt on him, beat him up something rotten, and left him for dead. As he lay there, he heard the sound of an approaching horse and rider, so he called out …

(Man stays on floor during the following action. Sound of hoof-beats is heard. Enter Sir Lancelot, knocking two coconut shells together to make the sound.)

MAN: Help, help! I've been mortally wounded!

NARRATOR THREE: The knight turned out to be none other than Sir Lancelot of the Round Table!

MAN: Hey, I know them, don't they do things for charity?

NARRATOR TWO: Oh yes! My Dad won the sponsored welly throwing competition last year. He threw it so far across the school playing field that it nearly went crashing through the caretaker's hut window!

MAN: Oh yes, I remember that. Who was it whose welly got stuck up a tree so that we had to get a long ladder to get it down? It must have been a right wally who threw it up there!

NARRATOR TWO: You could say he was a 'welly wally'!

(Laughter)

NARRATOR THREE: Uhuumm! Will you two shut up? I'm trying to tell a story. The Round Table was a group of special knights, loyal to King Arthur, and the present day fund-raising group gets their name from them.

SIR LANCELOT: As it happens, the person who threw the welly was very gifted and probably would have won, had it not been for a freak gust of wind at precisely the wrong moment.

MAN: Freak gust of wind? Hey, hang on a minute, wasn't it your Dad who threw that welly?

SIR LANCELOT *(Embarrassed, walks up to Man and gives a loud stage whisper to him, whilst aiming the tip of his sword into Man's stomach)*: Look, you're supposed to be mortally wounded, and if you tell anyone else that it was my Dad you certainly will be mortally wounded, OK?

(Returns to place, gives Narrators and Man a stern look, puts his sword away then smiles sweetly to the audience.)

NARRATOR THREE *(Looks fearfully at Sir Lancelot)*: Shall we continue? The Knight turned out to be none other than Sir Lancelot of the Round Table! Let's see if he stopped to help.

SIR LANCELOT: My dear fellow, what a dreadful mess thou art in! Unfortunately, I am on my way to have my armour re-fitted, it's become a little tight from all the banquets I have to attend. Any other time and I'd stop and help, you

know, but really I must be going. Good day!

NARRATOR ONE: Some good knight he was! The next person to arrive on the scene was a passing Bishop.

(Bishop arrives)

MAN: Help, help! I've been very mortally wounded!

BISHOP: Oh! you poor wretched creature! To what terrible depths you must have sunk for this to have happened to you. No doubt God is punishing you for something dreadful that you've done. Of course, it would be impossible for me to help you – I'm on my way to Rome to discuss the needs of the poor and needy – be of good cheer! Onward!

NARRATOR ONE: What a warped view of God he had!

NARRATOR TWO: Surely someone must have helped him.

NARRATOR THREE: Well let's see. The next person to travel along the road that day was an ordinary sort of bloke. But he wasn't from Wessex, he was from West Wales! The Man knew he was from West Wales even before he saw him because he could smell the leeks, but he was so desperate that he forgot his prejudice and cried out for help …

(Person from West Wales enters with leeks sticking out of pockets, Man and Narrators hold their noses as he/she speaks.)

MAN: Help, help! I've been very seriously morally wounded!!

WEST WALESER: Why, my poor fellow! You've been attacked! Let me clean your wounds up for you.

NARRATOR THREE: He tried to stand him up, but he was in no fit state, so he put him on his donkey and led him off to a local inn.

NARRATOR ONE: He gave the inn-keeper some money and a couple of leeks, and asked him to look after the man until he was well enough to go home again.

NARRATOR TWO: Both the inn-keeper and the man who had been robbed were so amazed by the kindness of the man from West Wales. He had shown mercy and kindness, whereas their own countrymen did not want to get involved at all.

NARRATOR THREE: Sir Lancelot and the Bishop may have pretended to care … *(Re-enter Sir Lancelot and Bishop)* but words must be followed up with actions. How can we say we are concerned when we do nothing to prove it?

(Everyone freeze.)

Discussion questions

1. Which Bible story does this sketch remind you of? (The Good Samaritan. Read it with the group – Luke 10:29–37)

2. Today, 'The Samaritans' is an organisation set up to help people, and is viewed as a good group. When Jesus told this story, the Jews hated the Samaritans, and thought they were the lowest of the low. Who gets pushed out, hated and mistrusted in our society?

3. Why do some people find it difficult to accept others from other areas of the country or of the world?

4. We may know that we are supposed to love and care for other people, even those we don't naturally like, but how do we change the way we feel inside?

Spend some time quietly thinking about your own attitudes to others, and ask God to help you change them if necessary.

God cares

What do you reckon is the worst thing that has happened to you? (Maybe it is still happening.) Write down what it was.

....

Remember the story of Ruth? This is what God said to her:

I'm here with you

I care

Let's see what we can do to bring some good out of things

1 OK, so what disasters happened to Ruth? Get out your Bible, look up the references and think of a word to describe what the situations were.

Ruth 1:1,2 ....
this meant poor health and physical pain

Ruth 1:5 ....
this meant mourning and sadness

Ruth 2:7 ....
this meant that life was hard

Ruth 2:7 ....
this meant loneliness and home sickness

2 Choose one of the four situations above. Imagine you're Ruth writing a letter to God about it. Remember where it comes in the story, think yourself into the character.

What would make the situation specially hard to cope with?

Dear God,

Love, Ruth

3 Try to write in this box all the good things that God did for Ruth, There are lots so you may have to cram them all in! Look up these references if you need a clue. Ruth 2:9, 2:14–16, 4:10, 4:13, 4:18

4 Rewind to the beginning. Did God mean the the things he said? It all worked out for Ruth, but it wasn't much fun at times. God makes those promises for us. Maybe you'll still have to wait to see good things come from the situation you wrote at the top.

Introduction

In a group of young people there will often be some who have experienced suffering in some form or other. In some cases you may know about this, for instance if a close relative has died recently, or if there is handicap, illness or other hardship in the family. In other cases it may be unknown, eg if a child has suffered, or is suffering, abuse, whether physical, sexual or emotional. You will need to be very sensitive in dealing with the subject of suffering. Here are some basic do's and don'ts:

- **Do** be alert to any children who are reacting badly to this topic.
- **Don't** offer glib answers or unspecific words of comfort, such as 'God will help you'.
- **Do** provide opportunities for children to speak privately with you, without feeling cornered, about their own hurts. One of the most helpful things you can do is *listen*.
- **Don't** give the impression that suffering is always the result of sin.
- **Don't** give the impression that if prayer for healing hasn't been answered it's because of sin, or lack of faith.
- **Do** show your own love and care for everyone in the group – whatever they may have experienced – and through that, convey God's love.
- **Don't** be afraid to look for professional help if there are situations you can't handle.

Activity (10 minutes)

You will need: strips of paper (about a quarter the size of A4) and pencils for each group member.

Explain to the group that they are going to play a game along the lines of 'Consequences', but serious rather than funny. Give a pencil and piece of paper to each group member and ask them to think of a form of suffering and write it at the top of their paper. When they have done that, get them to fold the paper over to hide what they've written, and pass it on to the person on their left. When the next piece of paper is passed to them, get them to think of a different type of suffering, write that down and fold the paper over again. Keep doing this around the group until it's obvious they have run out of ideas. The list below might help to prompt their thinking if they're stuck, and broaden their concept of the subject.

Suffering takes many different forms:

• Illness	• Malnutrition	• Bereavement
• Poverty	• Accidents	• Terrorism
• Unemployment	• Homelessness	• War
• Famine	• Natural disasters	• Cold
• Handicap	• Starvation	• Homesickness
• Loneliness	• Bullying	• Divorce
• Prejudice	• Persecution	• Pain

When the group members have finished, get them to open up their slips of paper and read them out in turn around the group. As each type of suffering is mentioned, it should be crossed off other people's lists, so that the same thing is not read out more than once. Point out that suffering can take many different forms. If appropriate, ask the group members to select one type of suffering from their list and to pray quietly for the people who suffer in that way.

Bible focus (20 minutes)

Briefly tell the group the story of Ruth. The headings in the Good News Bible will help you focus on the highlights. You could quote the following verses as you reach the appropriate points in the story: Ruth 1:3–5 – Naomi, Orpah and Ruth are all widowed; Ruth 1:7–9,16–18 – Ruth promises to stay with Naomi; Ruth 2:3,19, 20 – Ruth 'happens' to meet Boaz, who looks after her; Ruth 4:13–16 – Boaz and Ruth marry.

Give each member a 'God cares' sheet, a pen and a time limit of, say, ten minutes to complete it. If appropriate, have some feedback on what the group members learnt. Finish by reading Psalm 139:1–18.

Activity (10 minutes)

You will need: Bibles, and the following Bible verses copied onto cards and placed around the walls.

Sin came into the world … and brought death with it. As a result, death has spread to the whole human race because everyone has sinned (Romans 5:12).

The LORD's unfailing love and mercy still continue. The LORD is all I have, and so I put my hope in him (Lamentations 3:22,24).

Thanks be to God who gives us the victory through our Lord Jesus Christ! (1 Corinthians 15:57).

God teaches men through suffering and uses distress to open their eyes (Job 36:15).

Those who suffer because it is God's will for them, should by their good actions trust themselves completely to their Creator (1 Peter 4:19).

If God is for us, who can be against us? Who then can separate us from the love of Christ? Can trouble do it, or hardship or persecution or hunger

or poverty or danger or death ... nothing
will ever be able to separate us from his love
(Romans 8:31,35,38).

The aim of this activity is to show the group members that we don't really understand why people have to suffer (although some suffering is caused by people disobeying God) but that we *do* know that God loves us and cares about us and can bring good out of our suffering.

Ask the group members to stand in the middle of the room while you read the following questions to them, one at a time. The group members have to answer the questions by running and standing next to the appropriate Bible verses, placed around the edge of the room. Get a group member to read out the verse before moving on to the next question.

(Make it clear that there are many other verses in the Bible which refer to suffering and that these verses are not the complete answer to the whole thorny problem. They've been selected to help us understand a little more about something we'll never understand fully!)

1. Why is there suffering?
2. Even though there's suffering, what goes on for ever?
3. How do we know evil can't win?
4. Can there ever be any purpose in suffering?
5. What does the Bible tell us to do when we suffer?
6. What fact can we be sure of when we are suffering?

Visiting speakers

If you have anyone in the medical profession in your church, or anyone else involved in social work or other caring professions, invite them to talk to the group about their work and to answer questions. Arrange for the group to find out what 'caring activities' take place in the area and then to discuss which they would like to find out more about, or be involved in helping with.

Suggested questions:
• What types of suffering do you come across in your work?
• What sort of action can you take to help the people who are suffering?
• How do you cope, when you are dealing with so much human suffering each day?

Activity (20 minutes)

You will need: pens and small, plain pieces of card for everyone, a Bible and the following list on an overhead projector acetate or large sheet of paper:
• Pretend nothing's happened and change the subject.
• Don't mention it at all, so they won't get upset.
• Make them a cup of tea.
• Tell them jokes to cheer them up.
• Talk to them to take their mind off it.
• Say, 'Come on, don't cry – it won't help.'
• Listen to them without interrupting.
• Let them cry as much as they want to.
• Tell them to pull themselves together.
• Listen to them some more.
• Don't be shocked if they are angry.
• Keep in touch by phoning or writing if you can't drop in on them.

Ask the group members to imagine that one of their close friends is suffering. Perhaps a relative is very seriously ill, or dying, or maybe someone they loved very much has died, or been killed. Or maybe they are suffering in a different way. Perhaps they have just been told their mum and dad are going to split up, or they have got to go and live in another country. Maybe one of their parents has lost their job, or they are being bullied at school, or they are ill themselves. Whatever it could be, ask the group members to think themselves into the situation, and then ask them to decide how they might comfort their friend.

Show the list to the group and ask them to decide whether the actions could be helpful or unhelpful. Go through the list and get them to put a tick or a cross beside each thing, depending on which they think it might be and then ask them to say why they thought it was one or the other.

Point out that the helpful suggestions can only be used as guidelines, and that everyone copes with suffering differently. Explain that sometimes, the best people to help are people who have 'been there' themselves.

Refer to the 'HELP! Bible verses to comfort you' sheet. Maybe make several photocopies to pin up around the room. Suggest the group members choose the one they find most helpful, copy it onto their piece of card, learn it and then keep it in their Bible. Finish by reading 2 Corinthians 1:2-4 and then pray for any group members who are suffering in any way, or get group members to pray for each other in twos or threes.

Bible focus (20 minutes)

You will need: an overhead projector acetate (or a large sheet of paper) and pen and Bibles, pencils and paper for everyone, and numbered slips of paper with the following Bible references written on them: 1. Acts 9:22–25; 2. Acts 13:49–52; 3. Acts 14:19,20; 4. Acts 16:20–24; 5. Acts 27:39–44; 6. 2 Corinthians 12:7–10.

Explain to the group the context of 2 Corinthians 11:23–29. Paul was driven to boast of his 'achievements' because false teachers had been telling the church at Corinth that he was not a true apostle. While the passage is being read aloud, get a group member to make a list on the overhead projector acetate of all the different kinds of persecution that Paul suffered.

Divide the group into six and give each small group one of the slips of paper with a Bible reference on. Explain that you want them to investigate Paul's claims by looking up the evidence recorded. (You might also like to have some references books available which give general information about the difficulties and hardships of travel in those days.) Give each small group time to look at their evidence and then ask them to report back on what they have found. Ask them to sum up their findings in a newspaper headline, if possible (eg Group 2: 'Let's get rid of these preachers!' or Group 4: 'Jewish teachers are severely punished!' – you may need to help the groups.)

Discuss together why Paul was prepared to go through all this hardship, persecution and suffering. He could have had an easy life, but chose to accept suffering rather than give up preaching about Jesus.

Help!

Bible verses to comfort you

My brothers, consider yourselves fortunate when all kinds of trials come your way, for you know that when your faith succeeds in facing such trials, the result is the ability to endure (James 1:2–3).

If you suffer because you are a Christian, don't be ashamed of it, but thank God that you bear Christ's name (1 Peter 4:16).

We know that trouble produces endurance, endurance brings God's approval, and his approval creates hope (Romans 5:3,4).

We know that in all things God works for good with those who love him (Romans 8:28).

Leave all your worries with him, because he cares for you (1 Peter 5:7).

The Lord says 'I will comfort you, as a mother comforts her child' (Isaiah 66:12–13).

My grace is all you need, for my power is greatest when you are weak (2 Corinthians 12:9).

God has said, 'I will never leave you; I will never abandon you' (Hebrews 13:5).

May God our Father give you grace and peace (Colossians 1:2).

Prayer ideas

Instead of having the usual list of people who need prayer, collect pictures or photos from newspapers or magazines of people who have special long-term needs, such as the very elderly or handicapped people. Add pictures of famine, disasters etc, and refer to the other victims of circumstances mentioned in the 'Consequences' game. Share the pictures out amongst the group members and ask each group member to pray for the person or people in their picture (or any others that have been mentioned). Explain that it doesn't matter that they don't know the particular people – God does. Also, that person is representing others in the same situation. This could be silent prayer if your group doesn't want to pray aloud, or the prayers could be written down first.

Then they can swop pictures and repeat. You could do this as many times as you wish so that everyone prays for several people.

You could also photocopy and use the 'Prayabout' sheet. Group members could read out the different comments before a time of silent prayer.

The long silence

At the end of time billions of people were scattered on a great plain before God's throne. Most shrank from the brilliant light before them, but some groups near the front talked heatedly – not with cringing shame but with belligerence.

'Can God judge us? How can he know about suffering?' snapped a pert young brunette. She ripped open a sleeve to reveal a tattooed number from a Nazi concentration camp. 'We endured terror, beatings, torture, death.'

In another group a Negro boy lowered his collar. 'What about this?' he demanded, showing an ugly rope burn: 'Lynched for no other crime than being black!'

In another crowd a pregnant schoolgirl with sullen eyes. 'Why should I suffer?' she murmured. 'It wasn't my fault.'

Far out across the plain were hundreds of such groups. Each had a complaint against God for the evil and suffering He permitted in this world. 'How lucky God was to live in heaven where all was sweetness and light, where there was no weeping or fear, no hunger or hatred! What did God know of all that men had been forced to endure in this world? For God leads a pretty sheltered life,' they said.

So each of these groups sent forth their leader, chosen because he had suffered most. A Jew, a Negro, a person from Hiroshima, a horribly deformed arthritic and a thalidomide child. In the centre of the plain they consulted with each other. At last they were ready to present their case. It was rather clever.

Before God could be qualified to be their judge, he must endure what they had endured. Their decision was that God should be sentenced to live on earth – as a man.

Let him be born a Jew. Let the legitimacy of his birth be doubted. Give him a work so difficult so that even his family will think him out of his mind when he tries to do it. Let him be betrayed by his closest friends. Let him face false charges, Be tried by a prejudiced judge. Let him be tortured.

At last let him see what it means to be terribly alone. Then let him die. Let him die so that there can be no doubt that he died. Let there be a whole host of witnesses to verify it.

As each leader announced his portion of the sentence loud murmurs of approval went up from the throng of people assembled.

When the last had finished pronouncing sentence there was a long silence. No one uttered another word. No one moved. For suddenly all knew that God had already served his sentence.

Books

Dead Cert (by Roger Day, published by Harvestime) is a story about how we react to someone who might have AIDS.

Far Side of the Shadow (by Peggy Burns, published by Harvestime) is a story about a boy facing the possible death of his grandfather.

Joy in the Morning (by Carol Marsh, published by Scripture Union) is about a girl's grief at her father's sudden death.

I Needed a Neighbour (by Patricia St.John, published by Scripture Union) is the story of a family in a famine-stricken African country.

Nothing Else Matters (by Patricia St.John, published by Scripture Union) is about the civil war in Lebanon.

Videos

Beyond Words When mime artists visit a hospital, they discuss pain and death with one of the patients. (28 minutes – CRP)

The Hiding Place The very powerful, true story of Corrie Ten Boom's internment in a concentration camp. (2 hours – CRP)

Joni True story of a girl paralysed in a diving accident. (2 hours – CRP)

Prayabout:
Suffering

Underline any of these statements (all from readers of **One to One** Bible notes) that help you say to God what you want to about suffering. Then use them to start your own prayers about it.

People close to me are hurting too, Lord ...

- My friend wants to speak up about God but she's too shy and it makes her feel sad
- One of my friends is always being called names
- My friend is suffering with rheumatoid arthritis
- My friend gets school phobia and has to take anti-depressants before going to school
- My brother's marriage is breaking down
- Lord, all the suffering in the world makes me sad
- People are starving in places like Ethiopia because of other people's greed
- In Albania people want to know God's word but aren't allowed to
- People are still being killed in Northern Ireland
- In the big cities of the world, thousands are homeless
- It's inside people. Everyone suffers

But there has always been suffering, like for those people in the Bible ...

- Jesus who died on the cross
- Stephen who was stoned for what he believed
- Job who lost everything he had
- Joseph who was sold by his brothers
- Some of the first Christians who were persecuted, put in prison, beaten and even killed
- John the Baptist who had his head cut off for telling the truth
- Please help the people who are starving and give them the strength to carry on
- Open our eyes to the way they're suffering so that we want to do something to help them
- Please stop the bombings
- Protect the homeless and help people to think very carefully before they run away from home
- Be with everyone who suffers
- Give me peace of mind
- Please let the world know you share in its suffering and that you care
- Let everything be right

But sometimes I can see the good that comes out of suffering ...

- We can be forgiven because Jesus died
- My friend had leukemia but is now getting better
- Brian Greenaway was a Hell's Angel, but now helps prisoners to know Jesus
- An American was being held hostage but, when he was freed, it strengthened relationships between the two countries
- Suffering can bring families closer together
- Egypt gained a lot from all that Joseph went through
- When people suffer and come through it, they can help others who are going through the same thing
- It can help people rely on God more

Anger

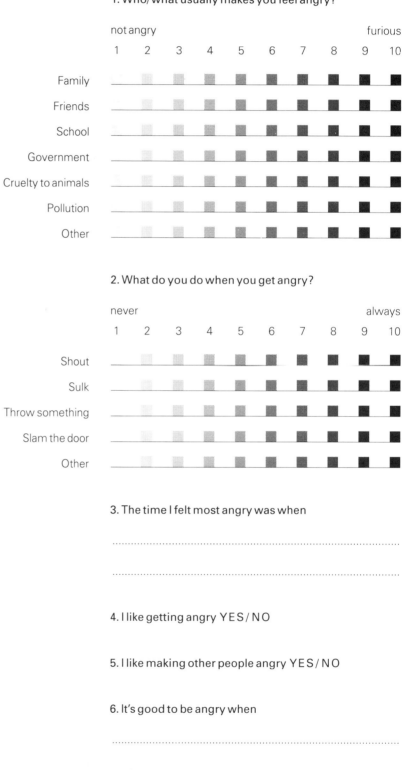

1. Who/what usually makes you feel angry?

	not angry									furious
	1	2	3	4	5	6	7	8	9	10
Family										
Friends										
School										
Government										
Cruelty to animals										
Pollution										
Other										

2. What do you do when you get angry?

	never									always
	1	2	3	4	5	6	7	8	9	10
Shout										
Sulk										
Throw something										
Slam the door										
Other										

3. The time I felt most angry was when

....

....

4. I like getting angry YES / NO

5. I like making other people angry YES / NO

6. It's good to be angry when

....

....

18. Violence

Introduction

Recent research has shown that children and young people are a lot more familiar with crime than adults think they are. A recent survey from the Centre for Criminology (1992) found that, within the previous year, 50% of the children interviewed had been victims of theft, assault or threatening behaviour on the streets. The media feeds us a relentless diet of violence, exploiting the fact that it fascinates our sinful, human natures. Far from being a remote issue for this age group, it is all too often a reality in their lives. The material examines the link between violence and anger and offers biblical advice in dealing with anger as a positive, as well as negative, emotion.

Icebreaker (3 minutes)

Before you start your meeting, brief two suitable group members to stage an angry scene as you are welcoming everybody. It doesn't need to be long or complicated, just a brief, heated exchange about something trivial. It does need to be convincing, though, so choose good actors and have a quick run-through in advance!

Welcome the group members to the meeting. The interruption will halt the proceedings. When it is over, without further comment read Proverbs 15:18 – 'Hot tempers cause arguments, but patience brings peace.' Explain to the group that it was a 'set-up' and ask them if they can guess what the theme for the meeting is! Explain that violence can be physical or verbal and that the group will be thinking about anger, hatred and revenge, what the Bible says about these things, and how Christians concentrate on forgiveness, reconciliation and peace.

Game (10 minutes)

Explain that this game illustrates the way in which most people encounter violence at a very early age. Divide the group in two and give each team three minutes to brainstorm on any children's fairy tales, nursery rhymes or cartoons which contain violence. (Examples include: Hansel and Gretel, Little Red Riding Hood, Three Blind Mice, and Tom and Jerry.) Have a quick game, whereby each group takes it in turn to call out the title of a story, rhyme or film which is violent. No repeats are allowed, and the winners are the group who can keep going when the other group has dried up!

Activity (8 minutes)

You will need: an overhead projector acetate or large sheet of paper and two different coloured pens, and a copy of a sensational type of tabloid newspaper!

Write the word 'Violence' in the middle of the sheet and then ask the group to brainstorm the word. Anything goes – write all their suggestions on the sheet, but avoid repetitions. You will probably get words like 'mugging', 'war' and 'hatred'. When all the ideas have dried up, ask the group members to look at the sheet and say how it makes them feel (eg depressed, sad, etc). *But …* those are the 'right' answers, which they will think you want! Tell them that and ask them to be *really* honest. Aren't they also fascinated by things like torture, cruelty and horror? Don't they find 'nasty' things attractive if they're honest? Quickly flick through the newspaper and provide some examples of the 'nastiness' which sells newspapers – it won't be difficult!

Now ask the group to think of opposites to the words on the sheet where possible, and write them in with a different colour pen, (eg forgiveness, peace, kindness, etc). Ask them to say honestly if those words seem a bit tame and boring. Now ask why it is that human nature is like that – they may or may not be able to tell you. Read Mark 7:21–23 and Romans 7:18–19, followed by Ephesians 4:22–24. Explain that God offers us the chance to change our natural, wrong attitudes and be forgiven by Jesus if we want to be – more details on request!

Activity (50 minutes or 25 minutes x 2)

Photostory

You will need: a Bible, a camera (with a flash if necessary), a colour-print film, and white sticky labels. (If possible, use a Polaroid camera – it's easier to have instant pictures, and avoids delay while the film is developed.)

Read Luke 10:25–37. Explain that Jews hated Samaritans, so when Jesus spoke about 'loving your neighbour' in this context, he really meant love your *enemies* (as in: 'Love your enemies, do good to those who hate you' [Luke 6:27]).

Explain that you would like the group to produce a photo story of this parable. They may prefer to put it in a modern-day context, with the 'victim' being a football supporter, for example, and the 'Samaritan' supporting a rival club.

You will probably find that the group take it from there of their own accord. It might be best if you appoint yourself as 'Film Director', to keep the proceedings under control! If you need them, here are a few guidelines:
  • Work out a storyline with the group. *Keep it simple.*
  • Decide how many shots are to be used and work on that number of scenes.

- Cast the roles.
- Use group members without an acting role as a source of props or costumes and as photographers.
- Set up each scene and shoot!
- When the pictures are available, arrange them in order.
- Compose 'speech bubbles' with the group (at most, two bubbles per picture).
- Get neat writers to write on the bubbles (cut out from white sticky labels).
- Stick speech bubbles on the photos and mount them on a large piece of card.

Story (4 minutes)

An article in the Radio Times describes two men of violence. One is an alleged leader of the Irish Republican Army, responsible for much bombing and killing in Northern Ireland. The other is a leading 'Loyalist', the Protestant backlash. which violently opposes the IRA. The article says:

'... the two men have many similarities. They are both young, working-class, church-goers, teetotal. Both are affectionate family men ...' But it goes on: 'Ostensibly nice people, there was a five-per-cent ruthlessness of personality. and when it showed it was frightening. They each had their own justification for killing people ...'

How do you react to such a mixed picture? Are they hypocrites, inhuman monsters who hide evil behind a church-going facade? It's hard to couple the respectable attitudes, the family affection, with the killing they both support. It seems so inconsistent.

Yet there's violence in each one of us. Most of us don't go around shooting to kill, bombing, maiming, but we react very strongly when people get in our way. We all have deep feelings of anger just waiting to surface, given half a chance. Violence is just under the skin, in spite of our commitment and protestations. We find it hard to come to terms with, and so we press it down deep into our sub-conscious; but it's still there. When it erupts we try to justify it, or blame the other person; so can these men of violence, that's what's so frightening about it. And we are all guilty of violence, in thought and word, if not in deed.

'... for everyone who hates his brother is a murderer' 1 John 3:15.

But when Jesus comes into the picture, the vision changes. He confronts the violence that's in all of us and takes it on himself. By refusing to respond in the same way, by offering love and forgiveness in the face of hate, he breaks the vicious circle of violent response. That's where life and freedom begin; not from the barrel of a gun, not from pride, but from a determined refusal to hate, and an acceptance even of our enemies as people for whom he died. It isn't easy. It wasn't easy for Jesus.

And with Jesus, it's not just a negative 'don't be violent' but a positive 'love your enemies, do good to them'. 'Yes, that's great theology,' say the cynics, 'but you can see it doesn't work in the real world.' Some of us would answer, 'How do you know? It's never really been tried.'

Activity (15 minutes)

You will need: a Bible, photocopies of the 'Anger' questionnaire and pencils for each group member and a copy of the 'Anger – good or bad?' chart on a sheet of paper or overhead projector acetate. The chart can either be completed or left blank for the group members to fill in.

Hand out the pencils and questionnaires and give the group members five minutes to complete them. Then get the group to split into twos or threes and compare results. Ask them whether they think anger is a good or bad thing. Quickly find out what each small group decided. (The answer is that it can be either, depending on the circumstances. It will be interesting to see if any of the groups come to that conclusion.)

Refer to the 'Anger – good or bad?' chart and either get the group to work out a negative and positive acrostic for the word 'A-N-G-E-R' or display the example, already completed. Ask the group to give examples of both (eg getting into an argument which leads to a fight, or demanding action for a victim of injustice). You could ask the group members to get into small groups, choose one of the examples, and make it into a specific situation with a short sketch. If they are stuck for ideas, use these scenarios:

1. Someone in a queue angrily accuses the person in front of them of pushing in and queue-jumping.
2. A disabled person is not allowed into a shop because their wheelchair would take up too much room.

	Bad	Good
A	Aggression	Achievement
N	Negative	Negotiation (working it through)
G	Grief	Gain new understanding (of self/others)
E	Exhaustion	Energy
R	Rebellion	Revolution (to change injustice)

Game (8 minutes)

You will need: two large cards, one with 'TRUE' written on it, the other with 'FALSE', stuck onto the backs of chairs and placed at opposite ends of the room.

Stand in the middle of the room with the group and read the following statements one at a time. When they have heard each one, the group members have to decide if they agree (true), or disagree (false) and run to the appropriate chair. It will make the group think – some of the answers can be either true or false, depending on circumstances. Discuss each 'answer' with the group.

1. Anger can lead to violence.
2. Anger should be expressed immediately.
3. I should never show anger. I should gradually let off steam in private.
4. God-given anger is meant to be used constructively.
5. Anger is a means of getting something off your chest.
6. Controlled anger can be a means of discipline.
7. It's ok to be really angry about some things.
8. Everybody gets angry sometimes.

9. Christians should try not to get angry.
10. You should never suppress anger.
Finish by reading Ephesians 4:26,31,32.

Outside activities

Why not suggest that some group members write to a prisoner of conscience?

Read the extract below about a card Terry Waite received whilst in captivity.

'I'll tell you a small story which I told in Damascus. I was kept in total and complete isolation for four years. I saw no one and spoke to no one apart from a cursory word with my guards when they brought me food.

'And one day out of the blue a guard came with a postcard. It was a postcard showing a stained glass window from Bedford showing John Bunyan in jail.

'And I looked at that card and I thought "My word Bunyan you're a lucky fellow. You've got a window out of which you can look, see the sky and here am I in a dark room. You've got pen and ink, you can write but here am I, I've got nothing and you've got your own clothes and a table and a chair."

'And I turned the card over and there was a message from someone whom I didn't know simply saying, "We remember, we shall not forget. We shall continue to pray for you and to work for all people who are detained around the world."

'That thought sent me back to the marvellous work of agencies like Amnesty International and their letter writing campaigns and I would say never despise those simple actions. Something, somewhere will get through to the people you are concerned about as it got through to me and to my fellows eventually.'
Terry Waite 19th November 1991

Lists of prisoners of conscience are available from:
   Amnesty International, Freepost, London EC1B 1HE
   Christian Solidarity International, 49b Leigh Hall Road, Leigh on Sea, Essex SS9 1RL

Videos

Balablok This wordless cartoon is a good discussion starter on human nature and aggression. (8 minutes – CRP)
The Cross and the Switchblade The true story of David Wilkerson's work amongst the gangs of New York. (100 minutes – CRP)
The Hiding Place The true story of Corrie Ten Boom held in a concentration camp for helping Jews to escape during the war. (2 hours – CRP)

Visiting speakers

You could invite someone from the Victim Support Scheme or the Prison Fellowship to speak to the group:
   Victim Support, Cranmer House, 39 Brixton Road, London SW9 6DZ. (071-735 9166)
This organisation has groups of volunteers around the country who visit and offer support to victims of crime.
   Prison Fellowship, PO Box 945, Chelmsford, Essex CM2 7PX. (0245 490249)
The main emphasis of the Prison Fellowship is prayer, for particular prisons, the prisoners themselves and the prison chaplains (who are responsible for the 'religious' side of prison life). They are also involved with writing to prisoners, befriending Christian ex-prisoners, and helping prisoners' families.

Prayer ideas

Ask the group to think of their 'enemies' – those people that they dislike, or can't get on with, or others who are mistreating them, or being cruel or unjust to someone else. Light a candle and read John 1:5 ('The light shines in the darkness, and the darkness has never put it out'). Suggest that, in the silence, the group members think of their enemies and ask God to help them forgive them, before praying for them by name.

Use prayers from prayer books which group members could select and read out. In particular, the well-known prayer of St Francis of Assisi, 'Lord, make me an instrument of your peace', would be appropriate and can be found in many different books of prayers.

The 'Prayabout war' sheet could be photocopied and used in small groups.

Poem (1 minute)

If a child

If a child lives with criticism, she learns to condemn.

If a child lives with hostility, she learns to fight.

If a child lives with ridicule, she learns to be shy.

If a child lives with shame, she learns to feel guilt.

If a child lives with tolerance, she learns to be patient.

If a child lives with encouragement, she learns confidence.

If a child lives with praise, she learns to appreciate.

If a child lives with fairness, she learns justice.

If a child lives with security, she learns to have faith.

If a child lives with approval, she learns to like herself.

If a child lives with acceptance and friendship, she learns to find love in the world.

Prayabout:
War

Use some of these suggestions to help you pray abut war. All the comments come from readers of **One to One** Bible notes.

> Lord, I'm not in the middle of a war right now and maybe I never will be. But all round me there are struggles that get nasty ...

- In Northern Ireland between Catholics and Protestants
- In my school playground, bullies and bullied
- In the government between the political parties
- At night in our town square
- When terrorists take people hostage
- At home in my family
- Strikes for more pay and picket lines
- Between people with racist attitudes
- Between crowds of football hooligans

> But recently, Lord, there have been major wars ...

- Between Iran and Iraq in the Gulf
- In Lebanon
- In the Falklands
- In what was Yugoslavia

> I don't really know what causes wars, Lord, but I guess it's that ...

- People feel the need to be superior and powerful
- The countries' leaders disagree
- People are greedy and jealous
- Deep down they're suspicious of each other
- Someone hurts someone else, and they retaliate a bit harder
- Arguments tend to grow and grow
- One belief goes against another belief
- Some people don't mind how much it costs to get their own way
- People are too proud to back down or compromise

> What really makes me sad about war is that ...

- They start in the first place
- People can't just live together in peace
- People are ready to kill (How do they have the nerve to fire death at other people?)
- The two sides could sort it out another way but won't
- People like my grandad are forced to fight
- People are scared and can't get to the shops
- Loads end up homeless
- It seems to on for so long
- Nobody seems to gain very much in the end
- Young men get blown up (Imagine how their parents must feel when they hear the news that their son is dead)
- Coffins and funerals are so expensive for poor families

> Lord, please ...

- Help all wars to stop and there to be no more hurt
- Help it calm down
- Don't involve me
- Make man too afraid to use nuclear bombs
- Get them to ban nuclear weapons
- Don't let there be World War Three
- Help people realise what they're doing to themselves by fighting and killing
- Help all the families and friends of the people who die
- Help people in future to sort things out by talking
- Show your peace in the whole situation
- Show everyone how nice it can be when people get on together